Foodie Tales

DESIRÉE MOORE

MASCOT® BOOKS

www.mascotbooks.com

Foodie Tales: A Family Cookbook Inspired by
Classic Children's Literature

Illustrations by Sara Brenton

For more information, please contact:
Mascot Books
620 Herndon Parkway #320
Herndon, VA 20170
info@mascotbooks.com

Library of Congress Control Number: 2020910221

CPSIA Code: PRTWP0720A
ISBN-13: 978-1-64543-124-4

Printed in Malaysia

For Johnny,
Poppy,
and Jude,
my loves

INTRODUCTION

When I was a little girl, I had a cookbook called *Kids Cooking*. It was a simple cookbook with a handful of fun, easy recipes. It was through this book that I first discovered my love for cooking—and brownies!—and I have been cooking for my family and friends ever since.

When my son Johnny was born, he loved books and reading from the start. When he was as little as six months old, he would reach for his books and nudge me to read all throughout the day. His love of books inspired my own renewed interest in children's literature, and together we have read whimsical, fantastical, imaginative books on subjects ranging from hungry caterpillars to whiny crayons to berserk hippos (and nowadays, lots of *Star Wars, Fancy Nancy,* and *Diary of a Wimpy Kid*!).

As soon as he was old enough, Johnny also loved to help in the kitchen. The very first thing we made together was chocolate chia seed pudding. We made it in a big silver bowl while sitting on the floor of our kitchen, and that is one of my favorite memories of Johnny and me when he was still a little boy. When my daughter, Poppy, was born and old enough, we included her in our cooking as well. She loves to sit up on the counter with her feet dangling and help, and she has become my everyday partner in the kitchen, especially at dinnertime. Now, we all cook together on the weekends, and everyone in our family pitches in.

This book is a compilation of our very favorite things to make in the kitchen, inspired by our very favorite children's stories. Some recipes are literal, taken nearly from the pages of the books themselves. Others are interpretive, where we've read between the lines to extract a recipe that we think gets to the heart of the book. Together, it is a literary foodie mash-up! We hope you love it as much as we do, and we hope it inspires you to enjoy good food and cooking.

All of the recipes are meant to be prepared as a family, with everyone helping out. There are roles for everyone in each recipe, and you can assign tasks by reading the recipe first and deciding who will be in charge of what.

Finally, if you haven't yet read the stories referenced in this cookbook, please do. They are true treasures. You can buy them in stores or online, or ask the librarian at your school or local library to help you check them out for free!

A NOTE ABOUT YOUR HEALTH

We can't talk about food and cooking without also thinking about our health. It is the most important asset we have, and we have to preserve it. We can do this through exercise, healthy eating habits, and regular visits to a trusted doctor. Once you know what makes you feel your best, form good habits and stick with them. The following are a few easy, healthy habits to get you started.

DRINK LOTS OF WATER

Drink lots of water. Staying hydrated is important for healthy minds and bodies. Add freshly squeezed lemon, slices of cucumber, or whole berries to your water to make it taste more special.

Eat whole foods. Whole foods are those that are as close as possible to what they were like in nature. For example, fruits, vegetables, nuts, oats, and quinoa (pronounced "keen-wah") are whole foods—exactly as you would find them if you plucked them from the trees or fields yourself. These foods are pure, and have no added ingredients. They have not been processed or altered. You would be surprised, too, that if you buy whole, healthful foods in bulk—like oatmeal and brown rice—you can actually save money. If you are buying packaged foods from the grocery store, make sure to read the ingredients closely. The fewer ingredients listed, the better!

EAT THE RAINBOW

Eat the rainbow. At mealtime, try to identify at least four colors of the rainbow on your plate. For example, a great meal might include some combination of: (red) tomatoes or strawberries or apples; (orange) carrots or sweet potatoes; (yellow) squash or peaches; (green) bell peppers or peas or beans or asparagus or spinach; (blue) blueberries; and (purple) grapes or beets or plums. If you can't access fresh fruits and vegetables, frozen or canned fruits and vegetables with no additives (no sugar or salt/sodium or other unnecessary ingredients) are a very good option.

Buy organic produce when possible. While organic produce can sometimes be costly, look for local farmers' markets or community supported agriculture (CSA) boxes where organic produce can be purchased inexpensively. Also, be sure to wash all of your fruits and vegetables thoroughly before eating. The cleaner your fruits and vegetables, the better your insides will feel.

COOK AT HOME

Cook and eat homemade meals as often as possible. This is the best way to ensure that you are eating high-quality foods with the healthiest ingredients. By the time you even consider what you might order in a drive-thru or for takeout or delivery, you can have a simple and healthy meal prepared from the ingredients in your pantry. Cooking at home can also be less expensive than eating out. Use this cookbook to get you on the path to cooking healthful, inexpensive meals at home on a regular basis.

EAT LEAN PROTEIN

Incorporate lean meats and other proteins into your diet on a regular basis. Foods like high-quality, locally sourced red meat (on occasion); lean chicken and turkey; and fresh, wild-caught fish are excellent ways to get protein. Eggs, lentils, quinoa, oatmeal, and black beans are good sources of non-meat protein as well.

Keep your sugar intake to a minimum. It is fun to enjoy sweets on occasion, but be sure to do so in moderation and always in the company of family and good friends. The sweets you eat should be worth it—skip the sodas and candy and instead go for a small square of rich dark chocolate or a freshly baked pastry.

Be an adventurous eater. Try new foods with an open mind. You don't have to eat *all* of something, but you should *taste* everything, especially if it's something you've cooked yourself!

Keep healthful items on hand and make them part of your weekly grocery shopping routine. This way, you will always be able to pull together a quick, healthy meal right from your pantry, even at the last minute. The lists on the next page will give you some good guidance.

PREPARING YOUR KITCHEN

We like to keep healthful foods on hand throughout the week (and many of the recipes in this book incorporate everyday foods from our pantry). If you would like to do the same, use this chart as a guide.

REFRIGERATOR

Assorted fruits and vegetables

- asparagus
- beets
- berries
- broccoli
- carrots
- cauliflower
- corn
- cucumber
- eggplant
- green beans
- leafy greens
- lettuce
- peppers
- radishes
- yellow squash
- zucchini

Milk

- almond milk
- cow milk
- oat milk
- rice milk
- soy milk
- any other milk that works best for you and your family—but be on the lookout for (and avoid) added sugars in non-dairy milk

Assorted cheeses

- blue
- cheddar
- goat
- Gouda
- Monterey Jack
- mozzarella
- Parmesan

Other

- butter
- corn tortillas
- eggs
- whole grain bread and pita
- whole milk yogurt

FREEZER

Assorted frozen fruits and vegetables

- berries
- broccoli
- mango
- peaches
- peas
- pineapple
- spinach

Assorted raw nuts*

- almonds
- hazelnuts
- pine nuts
- walnuts

nuts are high in fat and tend to spoil if not frozen

PANTRY

Assorted other produce

- garlic
- onions
- potatoes
- shallots
- squash
- sweet potatoes

Assorted low salt/sodium, no sugar added canned goods

- black beans
- garbanzo beans
- kidney beans
- pinto beans
- whole peeled tomatoes

Oils and vinegars

- apple cider vinegar
- balsamic vinegar
- canola oil
- olive oil
- peanut oil
- red wine vinegar
- rice wine vinegar
- sesame oil
- vegetable oil

Assorted low salt/ sodium stocks and broths

- beef broth
- chicken broth
- vegetable broth

Assorted whole wheat and regular pasta

- elbow
- penne
- rotini
- shell
- spaghetti
- tiny stars

Assorted baking ingredients

- baking powder
- baking soda
- cinnamon
- cocoa powder
- flour (all purpose, wheat, almond, coconut)
- honey
- sugar (white, brown, powdered)
- vanilla

COUNTERTOP

Assorted fruits

- apples
- avocados
- bananas
- lemons
- limes
- oranges
- peaches
- pears
- plums
- tomatoes

Fresh herbs in pots

- basil
- cilantro
- mint
- parsley

If you don't have all of these items in your pantry right away, that's okay. Focus on the fresh ingredients first, and the refrigerated items next. You can make a lot of these recipes with those two categories of items alone, and you can stock your pantry slowly with the remaining items over time.

KITCHEN RULES

Before we begin, let's discuss a handful of kitchen rules and other safety concepts that will serve you well as you make the recipes in this book.

Always cook with adult supervision, and ask an adult for assistance when using knives and electronics, or when preparing a recipe that requires the use of a stove or oven.

Before you begin cooking, **wash your hand thoroughly**, and wash your hands as you go. This will reduce unwanted germs that can be transmitted in the kitchen as you are handling raw and unwashed foods.

Read each recipe in full before you start. This will reduce the number of mistakes you make. This will also help you get organized and assign tasks. Once you have read the recipe, collect your ingredients, measure them as directed, and line them up in the order in which you will need them so that you can prepare the recipes easily.

Clean your workspace as you go. There is nothing worse than cooking with a big mess all around you. Keeping your workspace clean, just like hand washing, also ensures that you do not contaminate your food with things that should not be in there. Finally, if you clean as you go, you will have less to do at the end, and more time to enjoy what you have prepared!

Take extra precautions when working with ingredients that can be potentially harmful if not handled or cooked properly. An adult assistant should be on hand to help you handle raw meat, poultry, fish, and eggs, for example, so that your workspace and your food do not become contaminated.

SOME "HOW-TO'S"

How to Decipher the Measurements in Recipes

C = Cup
T. = Tablespoon
t. = Teaspoon
oz. = Ounce
lb. = Pound

How to Pick "High-Quality" Ingredients

A number of the recipes indicate that you should use "high-quality" ingredients like "high-quality vegetable stock," "high-quality ham," "high-quality peanut butter," and more. Please note that we recommend that you use quality ingredients across the board whenever you can. As used in the recipes, however, "high-quality" means you should take extra care to ensure the ingredient is fresh, local, organic, and made with the fewest ingredients possible and with no unnecessary additives like salt/sodium, sugar, corn syrup, or other sweeteners. If you are not sure where to start, ask someone who works in your local grocery store for help.

How to Cook Pasta

Unless a recipe directs otherwise, pasta should be cooked in rapidly boiling water that has been generously salted. When prepared properly, pasta should be firm and have a bite to it (this is called "al dente" in Italian, which means "to the tooth"), and it should stand up to any sauce that it is dressed with. Pasta is overcooked if it is soft or mushy, or if it falls apart in the sauce.

How to Chop Vegetables (and Other Ingredients)

A good number of the recipes in this book call for pre-chopped vegetables as key ingredients. The recipes will say, for example, "½ onion, finely chopped." Take time to do any chopping before you start so that you are organized and can jump into the recipe when you are ready.

Here are some tips for chopping vegetables and other ingredients in various ways:

Chopped: If a recipe calls for "chopped" ingredients, this means cutting the ingredients into somewhat uniform, bite-sized pieces with large, controlled strokes of the knife.

Roughly chopped: If a recipe calls for "roughly chopped" ingredients, this means cutting the ingredients into bite-sized, non-uniform pieces.

Finely chopped: If a recipe calls for "finely chopped" ingredients, this means cutting the ingredients into small, "fine" pieces, using the knife with precision.

How to Prepare Herbs

A handful of recipes call for herbs, either fresh or dried. Dried herbs are fairly self-explanatory, though it's interesting to note that recipes require fewer dried herbs than fresh herbs because dried herbs have a stronger, more concentrated flavor.

When preparing fresh herbs, handle them gently because they are delicate. To clean, rinse them under slowly running cold water and dry them gently in a thin, clean dishcloth or paper towel.

To extract the leaves, gently remove them from the stems (the stem of most herbs, like rosemary and thyme, are too tough to eat). To chop, spread them out on a cutting board and run your knife like a seesaw back and forth across the herbs until they are uniformly and finely chopped. You should have one hand on the knife handle and the other on top of the knife to avoid cutting your fingers.

Note that in some instances, the recipe will direct you to roughly chop the herbs, in which case you can tear them up with your hands to make things simple—a perfect job for kids to take on!

Miscellaneous How-To's

Grated cheese: A number of recipes call for grated cheese. While there are many pre-grated options on the market, I always opt to grate my own cheese. It doesn't take much time and you will avoid the additives and other unnecessary ingredients found in pre-grated cheeses that are included to prevent caking and clumping.

Broth: Several recipes call for broth, specifically chicken or vegetable. In each instance, you can use either homemade or high-quality store-bought broth. If you are making homemade broth, below are some tips.

For chicken broth, in a large stockpot, combine the bones of leftover chicken (I use the bones of a roasted chicken) with any vegetables and herbs you have on hand (celery, carrots, onion, and tomato, plus parsley, rosemary, bay leaves, and thyme). Cover completely with water. Bring to a boil and then reduce to a medium-low heat so that the water continues to simmer. Add salt and pepper to taste. Place a lid loosely over the top so the pot is mostly covered, but the steam can release. Stir the broth periodically and skim the white foam that rises to the surface. After several hours, take the broth off the stove, strain, and either use or store in an airtight container in the refrigerator for two to three days. (You can blend the strained vegetables with a touch of olive oil, salt, and pepper, and serve over pasta, meat, or fish.)

For vegetable broth, in a large stockpot, heat two to three tablespoons of olive oil over medium heat. Add a combination of whole vegetables and herbs of your choosing to the oil, including celery, carrots, onion, tomatoes, garlic, and shallots, plus parsley, rosemary, bay leaves, and thyme. Sauté the vegetables and herbs in the oil for several minutes, until the skins take on a little color. Cover completely with water and bring to a boil. Reduce to a simmer. Add salt and pepper to taste. Place a lid loosely over the top so the pot is mostly covered but the steam can release. Stir the broth periodically. After several hours, take the broth off the stove, strain, and either use immediately or store in an airtight container in the refrigerator for four to five days.

Measuring honey: We use honey in a lot of our recipes. As a tip, before you squeeze or scoop honey into a measuring spoon or cup, lightly spray the measuring instrument with cooking spray. This allows the honey to slide out more easily, and ensures that a layer of honey at the bottom does not get left behind.

RECIPE KEY

Easy: If a recipe is marked "easy," it can be completed in 30 minutes or less, and will require minimal adult assistance.

Medium: If a recipe is marked "medium," it will be slightly challenging, but can generally be completed in under an hour and will require some light to medium adult assistance.

Hard: If a recipe is marked "hard," it will take over an hour and will require the full attention of an adult assistant. These recipes are a challenge, but worth the work!

Adventurous: Recipes that are easy, medium, or hard may also be "adventurous" in flavor. We think these are the recipes you will end up loving the most, so don't be afraid to try them out!

AA: An adult assistant will be needed to complete the recipe. Depending on your age, most—if not all—of the recipes will require some level of adult assistance. Still, in each recipe there are lots of great ways for kids of all ages to help.

D: The recipe contains dairy. Unless the recipe says otherwise, anytime you see "milk," you can use your choice of whole, reduced fat, soy, almond, oat, coconut, or any other milk.

CONTAINS DAIRY

G: The recipe contains gluten.
(If a gluten-free alternative is possible, it is noted in the recipe.)

CONTAINS GLUTEN

GF: The recipe is gluten-free.

GLUTEN FREE

K: The recipe requires the use of a knife.

KNIFE

M: The recipe contains meat.

CONTAINS MEAT

N: The recipe contains nuts.

CONTAINS NUTS

N(O): Nuts are an optional ingredient.

O: The recipe will involve the oven.

OVEN USE

S: The recipe will involve the stove.

STOVE USE

V: The recipe is vegetarian.

VEGETARIAN

VE: The recipe is vegan.

VEGAN

All of these recipes are designed to be done as a family, and each recipe includes a number of ways kids can actively participate. For example, any measuring, stirring, or mixing is a great task for kids of all ages, and a great way for them to work on math skills, too! Older kids may be able to safely assist with cracking eggs, chopping fruits and vegetables, using the blender, and overseeing items on the stove with close supervision. As always, parents should use their best judgment when working with children in the kitchen.

CONTENTS

BREAKFAST & BRUNCH RECIPES

BOWL FULL OF MUSH

Serves 2–3 | Easy | AA | D | GF | K | N(O) | S | V | VE (if using non-dairy milk)

We have read Margaret Wise Brown's magnificent book, *Goodnight Moon*, so many times that the edges of the book have begun to fray and the pages stick together sometimes from things little hands have smashed into it. We love the cozy red and green room, the cows that jump over the moon, and the little bowl of steaming mush on the table. For this book, and as a way of bringing this story to life, we created our own version of a bowl full of mush: a fruity, crunchy, belly-filling dish that your whole family will love.

Ingredients

2 C water

1 C old-fashioned rolled oats

A pinch of salt

¼ C roughly chopped berries like blueberries, strawberries, and/or raspberries

¼ C roughly chopped peaches

1 t. cinnamon

½ C milk

⅓ C roughly chopped raw nuts like walnuts, pecans, and almonds, mixed (optional)

⅓ C roughly chopped dates and golden raisins, mixed (optional)

A touch of honey or maple syrup (optional)

Directions

1. In a medium-sized saucepan over medium heat, bring the water to a boil. Add the oats and salt and stir carefully. Cook the oats until the water is nearly absorbed, approximately 5 minutes. Every minute or so, stir the oats to ensure they are not sticking to the bottom of the pan.

2. Reduce the heat to low. Add the berries, peaches, and cinnamon and cook for another minute or so, until the fruit is warmed through but not mushy. Take the oatmeal off the heat. Scoop into bowls.

3. Pour a few tablespoons of milk over the top of each serving and sprinkle with a spoonful of nuts, dates, and raisins, and a drizzle of honey or maple syrup, if using. Serve warm.

Peaches are in season—and at their best—in summer months. If you are preparing this recipe during an off-month and cannot find juicy, ripe peaches, frozen peaches thawed to room temperature make a good substitute.

The most satisfying oatmeal inspired by *Goodnight Moon* by Margaret Wise Brown

LITTLE SAL'S BLUEBERRY MUFFINS

Makes 10–12 medium muffins | Medium | AA | D | G | O | V

We love the tone of the book *Blueberries for Sal*. It is a sweet, quiet story about two mothers (one bear, one human) and their blueberry-gulping children. It is a blueberry picking fantasy that leaves us with dreams of picnic baskets overflowing with plump sweet berries—and what better use of blueberries than for blueberry muffins? These muffins incorporate many of our favorite healthy ingredients, but still result in the juiciest, sweetest, and most indulgent muffins. Try to resist eating all the blueberries before you get around to making the muffins!

Ingredients

4 T. coconut oil, melted, plus more for coating the muffin tin

⅓ C softened cream cheese

¼ C milk

1 egg

1 t. vanilla

⅓ C honey

1 C old-fashioned rolled oats

¾ C whole wheat flour

1 t. baking powder

½ t. baking soda

¼ t. cinnamon

¼ t. ginger powder

¼ t. salt

1½ C blueberries

1 T. lemon zest

Directions

1. Preheat the oven to 375°F. Coat a 12-cup muffin tin with coconut oil. Set aside.

2. In a large bowl, whisk together the cream cheese, milk, egg, vanilla, and honey until smooth.

3. In a separate bowl, mix together the oats, flour, baking powder, baking soda, cinnamon, ginger powder, and salt.

4. Add the wet ingredients to the dry ingredients, then add the remaining coconut oil, and stir until just combined. Don't overmix.

5. Add the blueberries and lemon zest and fold until distributed throughout. Try to keep the blueberries whole and intact!

6. Using a large spoon or an ice cream scoop, scoop the batter into the muffin tin. Bake for 20 to 25 minutes, or until a toothpick inserted into the center of a muffin comes out clean.

7. Let cool for a few minutes in the tin and then transfer to a cooling rack to cool completely. Split in half with your hands and enjoy with a small pat of butter in the middle.

> When zesting any citrus, zest the skin only, not the white pith, which is bitter. The best tool to use for this is a Microplane grater, but a small, fine grater will work too.

Sweet and soft blueberry muffins inspired by *Blueberries for Sal* by Robert McCloskey

I DO LIKE GREEN EGGS!

Serves 3–4 | Medium | AA | D | G | GF (without toast or with gluten-free bread) | K | M | S | V (without ham)

Green Eggs and Ham is everyone's favorite funny food book. There was no way we could do this cookbook without including it. We tried a few different recipes before landing on this one, and we think it would make Sam proud. The eggs are just green enough, they taste great, and they're healthy too. Pair the eggs with your favorite high-quality ham, and serve in large batches for friends and family on a lazy Sunday.

Ingredients

4 C uncooked baby spinach

6 eggs

½ C shredded white cheddar cheese (using white cheddar is best here so that the green of the spinach can really stand out)

2 T. olive oil

8–10 slices of high-quality ham of your choice (we like salami, thick cut country ham, crispy bacon, or Italian prosciutto—or skip the ham for a vege-tarian option)

Buttered toast (optional)

Salt and pepper to taste

Directions

1. Thoroughly wash the spinach. Add several cups of water to a large saucepan (there should be an inch or so of water at the bottom of the pan). Fit the pan with a steamer. If you don't have a steamer, a metal colander will work just as well. Bring the water to a boil.

2. Add the spinach to the steamer or colander. Reduce the water to a simmer, cover the pan, and steam until the spinach is soft and tender, about three minutes. Remove the spinach from the heat and let cool.

3. Once cool enough to handle, strain the excess water from the spinach using a fine strainer or cheesecloth (or even a paper towel in a pinch!). Press and squeeze until water stops running from the spinach. When the spinach is as dry as possible, transfer to a cutting board and carefully run a knife through it in various directions until it is finely chopped. Set aside.

4. Crack the eggs into a medium-sized bowl and beat with a fork or whisk until smooth. Add the spinach and cheese to the eggs and beat further, until all ingredients are well incorporated. Lightly salt and pepper the egg mixture to taste (you can add more later as needed).

5. In a nonstick pan over medium heat, warm the

olive oil for 2 to 3 minutes. While the olive oil is heating up, plate the ham and make buttered toast, if using. Add the egg mixture to the warm pan. Using a wooden spoon or silicone spatula, gently stir the eggs in a circular motion several times. Then, move the spoon or spatula gently from one side of the pan to the other, ensuring the eggs do not stick to the bottom. Continue this side-to-side motion for 3 to 4 minutes, or until the eggs are firm and fluffy and no liquid egg remains. Turn off the heat.

6. Serve immediately alongside ham and buttered toast, if using.

Just perfect "green" eggs and ham inspired by *Green Eggs and Ham* by Dr. Seuss

EVERYDAY BREAD AND JAM

Makes one large loaf of bread | Hard | AA | D | G | O | V

Makes 1–2 cups of jam | Medium | AA | GF | K | S | V | VE

In *Bread and Jam for Frances*, Frances the badger wishes for bread and jam for every meal. We really can't blame her! Warm, soft bread with lightly sweet and tangy jam is our idea of the perfect meal too. This recipe is great for breakfast, a midnight snack, and every meal in between (just don't forget to eat other stuff *sometimes* or you'll end up like Frances!).

Ingredients (for the Bread)

¼ C high-quality olive oil, plus more for coating the loaf pan

2¼ C all-purpose flour

1 T. baking powder

¼ t. kosher salt

3 eggs

1 C Greek or whole milk yogurt

½ C honey

Ingredients (for the Jam)

2 lbs. whole strawberries, washed and cut into fourths

½ C sugar

⅛ C freshly squeezed lemon juice

> This is not a recipe for long-lasting, processed jam that can be kept in a glass jar outside of the refrigerator. This jam should be refrigerated and eaten within days.

Directions (for the Bread)

1. Preheat the oven to 325°F. Using a pastry brush or your fingers, coat an 8½-inch loaf pan with olive oil and set aside.

2. In a large mixing bowl, combine flour, baking powder, and salt. In a separate bowl, whisk together the eggs, yogurt, remaining oil, and honey.

3. Pour the wet mixture into the dry mixture and stir gently with a spatula to combine. Stir until the ingredients are just combined. Don't overmix or the bread will become tough.

4. Pour the batter into the loaf pan and bake for 40 to 45 minutes, or until a toothpick inserted in the center comes out clean. Transfer to a cooling rack and serve once it has cooled slightly.

Directions (for the Jam)

1. Add the strawberries, sugar, and lemon juice to a saucepan over medium heat. Stir carefully until the sugar is fully dissolved. Slowly increase the heat and bring the mixture to a boil. As the heat is increasing, stir the mixture thoroughly every minute or so. Once it reaches a boil, reduce the heat to medium and allow the mixture to simmer and reduce for approximately 20 minutes. While simmering, use a wooden spoon to mash and break up the strawberries into the desired consistency.

2. Take the strawberry mixture off the heat and let cool. Place in a jar or other container and refrigerate up to 3 days.

Spongy homemade bread and fruity jam inspired by *Bread and Jam for Frances* by Russell Hoban

FLAT AS A RABBIT PANCAKES

Makes 10–12 medium-sized pancakes | Medium | AA | D | G | N | S | V

We were smitten from the start with the strange and silly book *The Flat Rabbit*, about a hard-thinking dog and nervous rat who find a flat rabbit in the road and contemplate what to do with it (told you it was strange and silly!). This book inspired our pancake recipe because it made us think of the phrase "flat as a pancake," except these pancakes are anything but flat. They are thick and fluffy with great texture and a little bit of sweetness from the honey. With some of our tried and true ingredients—whole wheat and almond flours, yogurt, and honey—they make a healthy start to any day.

Ingredients

2 C whole wheat flour

¾ C almond flour

¼ t. salt

4 t. baking powder

2 t. cinnamon

2 eggs

2 C milk

½ C Greek yogurt

2 T. honey

Cooking spray, or a touch of oil or butter

Directions

1. Combine the flours, salt, baking powder, and cinnamon in a large bowl. Set aside.

2. In a separate large bowl, whisk together the eggs, milk, yogurt, and honey until smooth. Pour the wet ingredients over the dry ingredients and stir gently until combined. Don't stir too much or too long or the pancakes will be chewy and tough.

3. Heat a griddle or pan over medium heat and lightly coat with cooking spray, oil, or butter. When hot, pour heaping scoops of batter down on the griddle or pan in a circular shape. Cook until the batter starts to bubble on top and the entire pancake lifts easily, about 3 to 4 minutes. Flip and cook on the other side until the batter is cooked through, about 2 to 3 more minutes. Repeat until you have used all of the batter.

4. Serve as they are ready, or keep the pancakes warm in an oven on low heat or in a warming drawer until the entire batch is done.

Easy griddle pancakes inspired by *The Flat Rabbit* by Bárður Oskarsson

MADELINE'S FRENCH TOAST

Serves 4–6 | Medium | AA | D | G | K | O | V

At a boarding school in Paris, France, twelve little girls "break their bread and brush their teeth and go to bed." The smallest one is Madeline, and we like how brave and spunky she is, so we dreamed up this French toast in her honor. It is a rich and delicious toast that we imagine tastes much better than the "bread" the girls actually eat, and we're sure Madeline would love it.

Ingredients

4 oz. cream cheese, softened

1 C fresh strawberries, diced

2 T. orange zest

4 T. honey

1 loaf Challah or other egg bread, thinly sliced

4 eggs

2 C milk

Juice of one orange, freshly squeezed

1 T. cinnamon

> When zesting any citrus, zest the skin only, not the white pith, which is bitter. The best tool to use for this is a Microplane grater, but a small, fine grater will work too.

Directions

1. Preheat the oven to 425°F. In a bowl, whisk together the cream cheese, strawberries, orange zest, and 2 tablespoons of honey.

2. Spread approximately 2 tablespoons of the cream cheese mixture onto a slice of bread. Place another slice of bread on top like a sandwich and set aside. Repeat until you run out of the cream cheese mixture and/or slices of bread. You should have approximately 6 to 7 sandwiches. Cut the sandwiches in half down the center. Set aside.

3. In a large bowl, using a fork, whisk together the eggs, milk, orange juice, remaining 2 tablespoons of honey, and cinnamon. Continue whisking until the mixture is well blended and smooth.

4. Pour approximately a quarter of the milk mixture into a 9x13-inch baking dish. Arrange the sandwiches in the baking dish—squeeze them in if you have to.

5. Pour the remaining milk mixture over the sandwiches. Using the back of a spatula, press the sandwiches down into the milk mixture gently. The milk mixture should just cover the sandwiches.

6. Bake for approximately 20 minutes, until the milk mixture is the consistency of custard and the bread is lightly toasted on top.

7. Serve immediately with your favorite sweetener, like maple syrup or honey (or add a dusting of powdered sugar or warm chocolate-hazelnut spread for something extra special) on top.

A special French toast inspired by *Madeline* by Ludwig Bemelmans

LITTLE SWEET POTATO HASH

Serves 4–6 | Hard | AA | D | GF | K | M (with sausage) | O | S | V (without sausage)

In the book *Little Sweet Potato*, a little sweet potato rolls out of his patch and goes in search of a new home. His difficult journey makes finding a home that much better. This recipe was inspired by the little sweet potato, and that feeling of home. With sausage and a soft egg, and sweet, crispy hash, this is homemade comfort food at its best (but please don't tell the sweet potato we ate him after all that!).

Ingredients

1 T. olive oil (use 2 tablespoons if you are opting for the vegetarian version)

½ onion, finely chopped

½ lb. high-quality ground sausage (pork and turkey sausage both work well—substitute tempeh, tofu, or seitan for a vegetarian version)

1 C kale, finely chopped

2 medium sweet potatoes, grated

Salt and pepper to taste

6 eggs

1 C cherry tomatoes, cut into fourths

½ C Parmesan cheese, grated

¼ C fresh herbs for sprinkling (any combination of basil, rosemary, and/or sage will work well)

Directions

1. Preheat the oven to 350°F.

2. In an oven-safe skillet, heat the olive oil on medium heat. Add the onion and sauté until soft and translucent, 5 minutes or so. Add the sausage to the pan and sauté on medium to medium-high heat until cooked through, 8 to 10 minutes. Make sure to crumble the sausage as much as possible (a wooden spoon works well for this). Using a slotted spoon, remove the sausage from the pan and put aside. Leave the oil from the cooked sausage in the pan.

3. In the same skillet, add the kale and sauté in the oil on medium heat until the leaves begin to wilt, 5 minutes or so. Add the grated sweet potato. Using a wooden spoon, distribute the sweet potato around so that as much of it as possible is touching the pan. Stir frequently and cook until soft and tender, approximately 10 minutes.

4. Take the pan off the heat and add the cooked sausage back in. Stir until the mixture is well combined. Taste for seasoning and add salt and pepper to taste.

5. Carefully crack all 6 eggs on top of the hash, spacing them evenly around the pan and taking care not to break the yolks. Sprinkle the cherry tomatoes all around.

6. Transfer the pan to the oven and bake until the egg whites are firm and the yolks are soft, 5 minutes or so. If you don't like runny eggs, bake the eggs a little longer, until the yellow center of the eggs firm up as well.

7. Remove carefully from the oven (use a pot holder for the handle and leave it draped over the handle so no one accidentally reaches for it). Add more salt and pepper over the eggs to taste. Sprinkle with Parmesan cheese and herbs. Serve warm in oversized bowls (each person gets at least one egg!).

A savory hash inspired by *Little Sweet Potato*

by Amy Beth Bloom

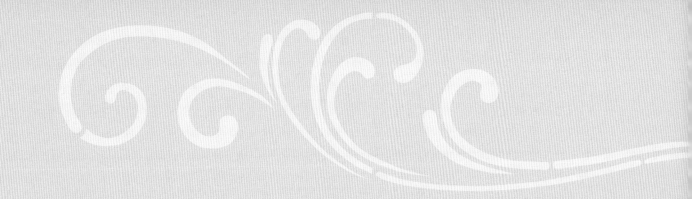

LUNCH RECIPES

BEST OF FRIENDS SANDWICHES

Serves 2 | Easy | D | G | GF (with gluten-free bread) | K | M

Frog and Toad is a beautiful series about, well, a frog and a toad who are the best of friends. They are kind to each other. They support each other and take care of one another when they need it most. These sandwiches honor the friendship between Frog and Toad (and would fit right into their picnic basket). The sandwiches are sweet, tangy, and a little surprising, and ideal when enjoyed with a best friend by your side.

Ingredients (Frog Sandwich)

2 T. sour cream

1 t. shallot, finely chopped

1 T. freshly squeezed lemon juice

1 t. high-quality olive oil

Salt and pepper to taste

2 slices wheat bread (you can use gluten-free bread if you prefer)

4–6 slices high-quality, thinly cut deli roast beef

2 thick slices sharp cheddar cheese

½ medium-sized tomato, sliced

Directions (Frog Sandwich)

1. In a small bowl, add the sour cream, shallot, lemon juice, olive oil, salt, and pepper, and whisk until well combined. Spread the sour cream mixture on both slices of wheat bread. Layer the roast beef, cheddar, and tomato on one slice of wheat bread. Top off with the other slice.

Ingredients (Toad Sandwich)

1 T. high-quality cranberry sauce

1 T. sour cream

1 T. horseradish (optional)

2 slices sourdough bread (you can use gluten-free bread if you prefer)

4–6 slices high-quality, thinly cut deli turkey

2 thick slices Havarti cheese

1 romaine lettuce leaf, cut into fourths

Directions (Toad Sandwich)

1. In a small bowl, combine cranberry sauce, sour cream, and horseradish, if using. Spread the sour cream mixture on both slices of sourdough bread. Layer the turkey, Havarti, and lettuce on one slice of sourdough bread. Top off with the other slice.

For best results, use a cranberry sauce that resembles a jam. You can buy this pre-made or make it yourself by following the directions on the back of a package of frozen whole cranberries.

A perfect pair
of sandwiches inspired
by *Frog and Toad* by
Arnold Lobel

GRILLED CHEESE FOR GRUFFALO

Serves 2 | Easy | AA | D | G | GF (with gluten-free bread) | K | S | V

The Gruffalo, a big monster with terrible tusks and claws and teeth and jaws, is on the hunt for a sweet little mouse to eat. The mouse is clever and has plans of his own, but we fear the Gruffalo may be back before long. That's precisely why we made this delicious grilled cheese sandwich. The bread is rich and buttery. The Gouda is creamy with a hint of natural smokiness, and acts as a perfect complement to the sharp bite of the cheddar. Slip the Gruffalo one of these, and he will be so happy, he'll forget all about eating sweet little animals for good!

Ingredients

1 C sharp cheddar cheese, grated

1 C Gouda cheese, grated

4 slices high-quality sourdough bread (you can use gluten-free bread if you prefer)

Unsalted butter, slightly softened so it is easy to spread

½ pear or tomato, thinly sliced (use either the pear or the tomato, not both; both are optional)

Pinch of sea salt

Directions

1. In a medium-sized bowl, combine the cheddar and Gouda. Set aside.

2. Arrange the bread side by side like two open-faced sandwiches. Using a butter knife, spread a thin layer of butter on both sides of each of the slices of bread.

3. Put generous helpings of the grated cheese mixture on one side of each of the sandwiches, pressing the cheese into the butter so it sticks. Add one layer of pear or tomato on top of the cheese, if using. Sprinkle some additional cheese on top of the fruit. Close the sandwiches.

4. In a pan, grill the sandwiches on medium-high heat until the bread is golden brown and crispy and the cheese is melted through. Sprinkle sea salt on top. Serve warm.

Gooey, buttery grilled cheese inspired by *The Gruffalo* by Julia Donaldson

HOT DOG TO GO

Serves 6 | Medium | AA | D (with cheese) | G | GF (with gluten-free buns) | K | M | S

Go, Dog. Go! is a quirky book about big dogs and little dogs and colorful dogs and dogs wearing fun hats. It's about as twisty and strange as our hot dogs (a specialty of my sweet husband), and we think the hot dogs are a perfect sidekick to the book. These hot dogs are easier to make than they look (though you will need an adult's assistance) and make for an all-around crispy hot dog with your favorite ingredients nestled inside. This hot dog will delight and surprise all your guests.

Ingredients

6 high-quality hot dogs

6 high-quality hot dog buns (you can use gluten-free buns if you prefer)

Any of your favorite toppings (optional): cheese, tomatoes, pickles, mustard, ketchup, et cetera

Chicago-style (optional): freshly sliced tomatoes, pickle spears, hot peppers, sweet white onion, and bright green relish

New York-style (optional): spicy, brown mustard and sauerkraut

Directions

1. Run a wooden skewer through each hot dog from end to end.

2. Using a small, sharp knife (like a paring knife), make one continuous cut in the hot dog, starting at the top and turning the hot dog while you cut on the diagonal. The cut should be a quarter-inch deep (through to the skewer), so the hot dog opens up but isn't too thin at any given point. Repeat until all of the hot dogs are spiral cut.

3. Cook the hot dogs according to the instructions on the package, either in a pan or on a grill. Using tongs, arrange the hot dogs so they fit inside the buns. Top with whatever toppings you desire and enjoy!

A twisty, twirly hot dog inspired by *Go, Dog. Go!* by P.D. Eastman

MR. MESSY NACHOS

Serves 3–4 | Easy | AA | D | GF | K | O | V

Mr. Messy—and the *Mr. Men and Little Miss* series overall—is a classic children's book that is as good today as it was when I was a little girl. Mr. Messy, in particular, is a pink ball of mess who calls on his tidier and cleaner friends to rescue him. In the meantime, we are over here making a mess of our own, with this easy to assemble, messy pile of pan nachos. These nachos are so good, with varying layers of flavors and textures, you won't notice that they look like a mess (and make a little bit of a mess too)! Many of the ingredients in this recipe are optional, but we would encourage you to go for them all—the more flavor in each layer, the better.

Ingredients

½ T. vegetable oil

1 C canned black beans, drained and rinsed

4–6 C high-quality blue or white corn tortilla chips

1 C fresh or frozen corn kernels (if frozen, bring to room temperature)

2 C sharp cheddar cheese, grated

½ C sliced canned black olives, drained and rinsed

¾ C sour cream (or Greek yogurt) (optional)

1 t. cumin powder (optional)

¾ C cherry tomatoes, cut into fourths

½ avocado, diced

½ C cilantro, finely chopped (optional)

¼ C jalapeño, finely chopped (optional)

¼ C high-quality homemade or store bought salsa (optional)

Salt and pepper to taste

Directions

1. Preheat the oven to 325°F.

2. In a small bowl, combine the oil and black beans. Add salt and pepper to taste. Mix well, mashing the beans here and there so they are broken down just a little bit. Set aside.

3. Using a large sheet pan, arrange the chips in a single, flat layer. Sprinkle generously with the bean mixture, plus corn, cheese, and olives. Place in the oven for 10 to 15 minutes, or until the cheese is melted and the beans and olives are warmed through.

4. In the meantime, combine the sour cream and cumin powder, if using.

5. Remove the nachos from the oven and top— *messily*—with the sour cream mixture and the remaining ingredients. Serve warm.

A messy pile of pan nachos inspired by

Mr. Messy by Roger Hargreaves

HAM AND CHEESE SPINS

Serves 2 | Easy | AA | D | G | GF (with gluten-free tortillas) | K | M

We came across this stunningly fantastic book, *Sparkle and Spin: A Book About Words*, by accident. Well, actually, we came across it backwards. We wanted to include a ham and cheese roll recipe in our cookbook, but we didn't have a corresponding book that inspired it, so we went looking for books about wheels and rolling and spinning until we found it—this perfect book. Dig into this book about words and illustrations while munching on a fresh and light version of a ham and cheese with tons of crunchy, good-for-you vegetables and a tangy dressing that you'll want to use on all of your other sandwiches, salads, and vegetables.

Ingredients

2 flour tortillas (we prefer whole wheat but any flour tortillas will work, including gluten-free options)

½ C cream cheese

4 slices high-quality, thinly cut deli ham

1 leaf romaine lettuce, cut in half horizontally and again vertically

½ medium-sized tomato, thinly sliced

½ medium-sized cucumber, cut into long, thin slices

½ bell pepper (your choice of red, orange, or yellow), cut into long, thin strips

2 T. high-quality olive oil

¼ T. balsamic vinegar

Salt and pepper to taste

Directions

1. Lay the tortillas out flat. Spread the cream cheese evenly across both tortillas. Layer 2 slices of ham on each tortilla. Next, layer the lettuce, sliced tomato, cucumber, and bell pepper evenly, making sure to spread the ingredients out so the tortilla is not heavier in the middle or on either side. The vegetables should all be aligned in the same, vertical direction. Set aside.

2. In a small bowl, combine the oil, vinegar, salt, and pepper. Whisk with a fork until well incorporated. Using a spoon, drizzle the dressing over the tortillas.

3. Roll—or spin—the tortillas up from one side to the other (roll in the direction the vegetables will roll up most naturally) and press down to seal them closed a bit. Slice into one-inch wheels and serve!

A fresh take on ham and cheese rolls inspired by *Sparkle and Spin: A Book About Words* by Ann Rand and Paul Rand

THE MAGIC SANDWICH

Serves 1–2 | Easy | AA | G | GF (with gluten-free bread) | K | N(O) (with a nut butter alternative) | V | VE (with vegan bread)

This cookbook took about three years to complete. In that time our oldest son, Johnny, learned to read, and he began to read chapter books and books that are a little bit more advanced than some of the stories that originally inspired this book. One of his favorites, *The Magic Tree House* series, follows Jack and Annie as they travel through time, meet fascinating real and imagined characters, and often save the day. At the end of one of their adventures in ancient Egypt, they run back home and right into their mom, who is preparing peanut butter and jelly sandwiches. We took this as inspiration for our own PB&J, a classic recipe with a little something extra—all together, you might even call it magic.

Ingredients

High-quality peanut butter

2 slices dense and seedy whole grain bread
(you can use gluten-free bread if you prefer)

Homemade jam

2 large strawberries, tops removed
and thinly sliced

Directions

1. Using a spoon, scoop and spread the desired amount of peanut butter on one side of the bread. Using another spoon, scoop and spread the desired amount of jam on the other.

2. Press the sliced strawberries into the peanut butter side, layering and overlapping the slices a bit so they fit. Close up the sandwich. Serve with a big glass of milk!

Peanut butter alternatives like almond and cashew butter work well here. A nut butter alternative like sunflower seed butter also works well. Choose a nut or nut butter alternative without added oils or sugars.

The perfect PB&J inspired by *The Magic Tree House* by Mary Pope Osborne

SNACK RECIPES

GIVING APPLES

Makes 30–35 chips | Easy | AA | GF | K | O | V | VE

We don't know what to make of the beautiful book *The Giving Tree* by the great Shel Silverstein. It is a classic, and we feel a lot of things after reading it. If it's an uplifting story or a sad one, we aren't sure. We can see it both ways, and we've spent a lot of time mulling it over. In the meantime, though, these sweet, spicy apples are the perfect accompaniment as your heart flutters around with this book.

Ingredients

3–4 crisp, organic apples

Juice of ½ lemon, freshly squeezed

1 T. cinnamon

¼ t. ginger powder

Directions

1. Preheat the oven to 215°F. Line a large baking pan with a silicone baking mat or parchment paper. Set aside.

2. Using an apple corer, core the apples. (If you don't have an apple corer, skip this step and remove the stem pieces and seeds with a knife after you've cut the apples into rounds.)

3. Slice about a quarter inch off the tops and bottoms of the apples to stabilize it for cutting. Using a mandolin or a knife, slice the apples into uniform, thin rounds, about ⅛ of an inch thick. Place the apple slices in a medium bowl.

4. Using your hands, toss the sliced apples with the lemon juice, cinnamon, and ginger powder until they are evenly coated. Arrange in a single layer on the baking pan.

5. Bake for 2 hours, flipping the apple slices every 30 minutes or so with tongs to be sure they are cooking evenly and drying well. The apples are done when they are golden and crisp like a chip.

Oven-dried cinnamon apples inspired by *The Giving Tree* by Shel Silverstein

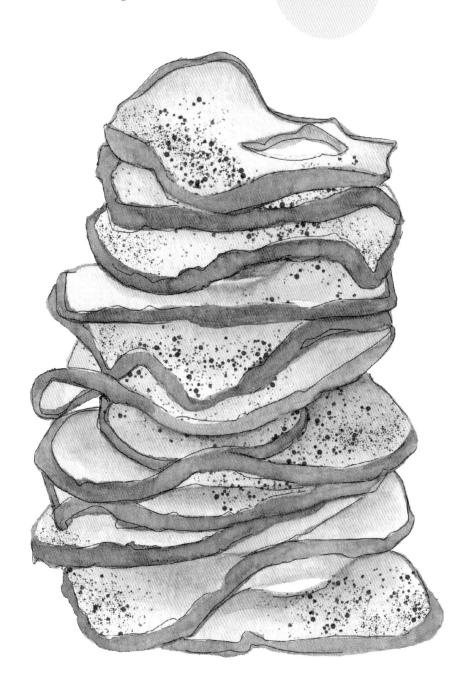

HUNGRY CATERPILLAR SNACKS

Serves many! | Easy | AA | D | G | GF (with gluten-free crackers and breads) | K | N(O) | V

The hero in *The Very Hungry Caterpillar* is the perfect inspiration for this recipe. He loves to eat and he eats all kinds of good stuff (all beautifully illustrated by artist Eric Carle). We took many of the foods the caterpillar ate on his journey through the book, and turned those into a fancy fruit and cheese plate. Arrange it however you like. Be creative. Make it abundant and imaginative. Share with lots of hungry friends!

Ingredients

1 apple, sliced

1 pear, sliced

A handful of dried plums, figs, or apricots

10 strawberries, cut in half with stems removed

1 orange or tangerine, peeled and broken into wedges

An assortment of your favorite cheeses, sliced or in large or small blocks (cheddar, Swiss, Brie, blue, Gouda, and goat are good options)

An assortment of crackers and homemade breads (you can use gluten-free options if you prefer, or a combination of both to accommodate all of your guests)

Honey

Assorted nuts (optional)

1–2 ounces of high-quality dark chocolate, broken into small squares

Directions

1. Arrange all of the ingredients on a large platter(s) or cutting board(s) in any way you like. Consider grouping the fruits together, followed by the breads and cheeses, followed by the chocolate. This show-stopping platter is fun to eat as a light dinner or pre-dinner party snack.

A collection of snacks inspired by *The Very Hungry Caterpillar* by Eric Carle

RAINY DAY POPCORN

Serves 2 | Medium | AA | GF | S | V | VE

The sun didn't shine and it was too wet to play when *The Cat in the Hat* showed up and made a big ol' mess with an assortment of things—from a cake to a gown to some milk to a fan to a ship to a fish! Personally, when we are stuck inside on rainy days, we like to take it easy and make popcorn instead, and maybe watch a movie or two. This popcorn recipe makes a perfect salty, crunchy snack, and it doesn't make all that much of a mess. (Kids under four shouldn't eat popcorn because it is a choking hazard, so keep this one away from younger brothers and sisters, please.)

Ingredients

3 T. coconut oil

⅓ C high-quality popcorn kernels

Sea salt to taste

Directions

1. Heat coconut oil in a large saucepot over medium heat. When the coconut oil melts, toss in one kernel and wait until it pops. When it pops, add the rest of the kernels to the pot and cover.

2. Lower the heat slightly and enlist an adult to pull the pot back and forth quickly and continuously over the heat. This shakes up the kernels and ensures that they cook evenly and don't burn. The kernels will pop rapidly. The popcorn is ready when the popping slows down to a few seconds between each pop.

3. Take the popcorn off the heat and pour into a large serving bowl (do this right away so the kernels don't burn from the heat at the bottom of the pot). Add sea salt to taste and gobble up (and afterwards, tidy up any popcorn that spills)!

Simply perfect popcorn inspired by *The Cat in the Hat* by Dr. Seuss

LITTLE ENGINE ENERGY BARS

Makes 6–8 bars | Medium | AA | D | GF | K | N | V | VE (with non-dairy milk)

A little engine helps a train car full of toys and food up and over a steep hill. The engine works hard, thinks positively, and is determined. We've always loved this book and the embedded lesson that you can do anything you put your mind to. As it turns out, the journey is even better if you can help others along the way. With a sweet snack full of natural sugars, protein, and a little cocoa powder for a kick, you'll surely have the energy to do both.

Ingredients

2 C dates, pitted and chopped

2 C raw cashew nuts

¾ C unsweetened cocoa powder

½ C raw almonds

⅓ C quick cooking oats

1 t. sea salt

3–4 T. milk

Directions

1. Place the dates, cashews, cocoa powder, almonds, oats, and sea salt in a food processor. Pulse until coarsely chopped. Add the milk 1 tablespoon at a time and pulse further, until the mixture forms a dough.

2. Place the dough in the center of a baking dish lined with parchment paper (a 9-inch square works well). Place a second piece of parchment paper over the bars, and press down evenly until the entire pan is covered. Remove the top layer of parchment paper and chill the dough in the refrigerator for 15 to 20 minutes.

3. Take the pan out of the refrigerator, lift the dough gently with the parchment paper and place on a cutting board. Cut into bars, approximately 2 inches wide by 3 inches long. These keep well in parchment paper in the refrigerator for 3 to 4 days.

CURIOUS BANANAS

Serves 1–2 | Easy | AA | GF | K (a butter knife will do) | N(O) (with a nut butter alternative) | V | VE

We have a feeling this snack would be just perfect for one curious little monkey who was adopted by the man with the yellow hat. It is also perfect for curious little kiddos. It is easy to make, healthful, and nutritious, and satisfying as a mid-morning or early afternoon snack. Add as much crunch as you like to this snack that will tide you over for any mischief you might get into after.

Ingredients

1 banana

2 T. high-quality nut butter of your choice

3–4 t. of coconut flakes

3–4 t. of sesame seeds

Directions

1. Peel the banana. Slice the banana in half vertically from top to bottom.

2. Use a knife or spoon to spread the nut butter or nut butter alternative across one side of the banana. Spread gently so the banana doesn't break. Using a spoon, sprinkle coconut flakes and sesame seeds on the nut butter or nut butter alternative. Close up the banana like a sandwich. Enjoy!

> Peanut, almond, and cashew butter all work well here—a nut butter alternative like sunflower seed butter works well too; choose one without added oils or sugars.

A rich and creamy banana and nut butter snack inspired by *Curious George* by H. A. Rey and Margret Rey

IT'S RAINING APPLESAUCE

Makes 1–2 cups of applesauce | Easy | AA | GF | K | S | V | VE

This is a beautiful book that reads like a poem, and the poem dreams up stars of lemon that rain applesauce. We've made a chunky, sweet, and tart applesauce as a tribute to the lemony stars of applesauce dreams. This recipe is great for children of all ages, including the littlest ones in the house, and works well as an accompaniment to both sweet and savory dishes.

Ingredients

2 C water

2 medium-sized apples
(organic apples are best), cut into big chunks

2 t. cinnamon, plus an extra teaspoon or so
for sprinkling

1 t. freshly squeezed lemon juice

Directions

1. In a medium pan, bring the water to a boil. Add the apple chunks to the boiling water and boil until tender. The apples are ready when you can pierce them easily with a knife. Retain 2 tablespoons or so of water and drain the rest. Set aside and let the apples and water cool.

2. When cooled, place the apples and water in a blender. Add the cinnamon and lemon juice. Blend until the apples reach a desired consistency—you can choose to make it more on the chunky side or more like a puree depending on your preference. Pour into serving bowls. Sprinkle with cinnamon and serve.

3. Store any leftovers in an airtight container in the refrigerator, up to 3 days.

Smooth and silky apple puree inspired by
Rain Makes Applesauce by Julian Scheer

TUESDAY GUACAMOLE

Serves 4–6 | Easy | AA | D (with cheese) | GF | K | V | VE (without cheese)

Tuesday is a book with no words; only pictures of bent clocks and deep swirls of blacks and blues, and also frogs—earthy green frogs. We don't know what to think, but we like it—almost as much as we like the earthy green guacamole that Tuesdays inspired. Make this guacamole on a Tuesday, or any day of the week, as a snack or side dish to round out a healthy meal. You can go with a plain or slightly more dressed up version depending on your preference. We go for all the toppings for a thick and chunky consistency that pairs well with our favorite tortilla chips.

Ingredients

4 ripe avocados

2 T. freshly squeezed lemon juice

6–8 cherry tomatoes, seeded and cut into fourths
(optional)

¼ C Cotija or feta cheese, crumbled (optional)

1 T. toasted pepitas (optional)

2 T. cilantro, roughly chopped (optional)

Salt and pepper to taste

Directions

1. Cut the avocados in half. Remove the pits and scoop out the flesh into a large bowl. Pour lemon juice over the top. Using a fork, mash the avocados and lemon juice until just broken down but still chunky.

2. Add the tomatoes, cheese, pepitas, and cilantro, if using. Fold the ingredients together gently, taking care not to break down the avocado or other ingredients too much.

3. Add salt and pepper to taste. Serve with blue corn or other high-quality tortilla chips.

An avocado is ripe if, after you remove the stem, the circle at the top is a medium, healthy green—not too light and not too dark.

Ethereal green guacamole inspired by *Tuesday*
by David Wiesner

GRANOLA ROCKS

Makes approximately 8 cups of granola | Medium | AA | GF | N | O | V

In *A Rock Can Be...*, we learn how special rocks are. Even ordinary ones can do and be extraordinary things. This granola, created by our dear friend Torey Halim, reminds us of varied rocks and pebbles (delicious ones, of course) and is a tribute to this clever and creative book.

Ingredients

6 C thick-cut oats

1 C pumpkin seeds

1 C sliced or slivered almonds

1 C chopped walnuts (or pecans)

½ C honey

⅓ C coconut oil

⅓ C pure maple syrup

1 t. cinnamon

½ t. nutmeg

½ t. salt

2 T. water

Directions

1. Preheat the oven to 275°F. Have a large baking sheet (with a rim) ready.

2. In a large bowl, mix the oats, seeds, and nuts. In a medium saucepan over medium-low heat, mix the remaining ingredients until the mixture is hot and well combined. Pour the wet ingredients into the dry ingredients and mix well. Using a spatula, spread the mixture evenly on the baking sheet.

3. Bake for 40 minutes. Take the pan out at the 20-minute mark and turn it so that the granola bakes evenly. After 40 minutes pass, check the mixture to be sure it is cooking evenly and slowly. Check the mixture every 20 to 30 minutes thereafter, stirring each time, until it is as golden and crispy as you like, approximately 1½ to 2 hours total.

4. Let the mixture cool before serving. Eat plain or serve with yogurt and fruit for a healthy, crunchy treat. Store any leftovers in an airtight container for up to 7 days.

Crunchy, sweet granola inspired by *A Rock Can Be...* by
Laura Purdie Salas

RUNAWAY CARROTS

Serves 2–3 | Easy | Adventurous | AA | GF (Check the ingredients in the tahini, because some store-bought tahini contains gluten as a thickener) | K (with cilantro or parsley) | V | VE

A little bunny explores his independence and imagines running away from his mother in all sorts of different ways, including becoming a fish in a trout stream, a rock on a mountain, and a crocus in a hidden garden. But his mother will find him no matter what, and when she does, she warmly offers him a carrot. In honor of this dedicated and loving mother bunny and her little runaway bunny, we have created a recipe that complements raw carrots—a creamy, tangy hummus for dipping.

Ingredients

1 can garbanzo beans or chickpeas (no salt/sodium or sugar added), drained and rinsed

¼ C tahini

3 T. fresh lemon juice

Salt and pepper to taste

High-quality olive oil for drizzling

A handful of fresh parsley or cilantro, roughly chopped (optional)

Paprika to taste (optional)

Raw carrots, sliced for dipping

Directions

1. Soak the garbanzo beans in water to loosen up the shells, at least 1 to 2 hours. Strain the water and use your hands to remove as many of the shells as possible (this is slightly labor intensive, but worth it as it gives the hummus a silky smooth texture). Rinse and set aside.

2. In a blender, combine garbanzo beans, tahini, and lemon juice. Blend until the ingredients form a smooth and creamy consistency. If you are having trouble blending due to the thickness of the bean mixture, add a tablespoon or so of water at a time until the mixture loosens. Add salt and pepper to taste and blend for another 10 to 15 seconds.

3. Pour into a serving bowl. Drizzle the garbanzo bean mixture with a touch of olive oil. Sprinkle with parsley, paprika, or cilantro, if using. Serve at room temperature, with carrots on the side. Store any leftovers in an airtight container in the refrigerator, up to 3 days.

> Tahini is a sesame paste popular in Middle Eastern cooking. You can find it in most grocery stores.

Carrots and creamy hummus inspired by

The Runaway Bunny by Margaret Wise Brown

DINNER RECIPES

MAX'S STILL-HOT MAC & CHEESE

Serves 4–6 | Medium | AA | D | G | S | V

We adore the beautiful, whimsical book *Where the Wild Things Are* by the brilliant Maurice Sendak, about a mischievous boy named Max who goes on an adventure with the "wild things." When he returns home from his adventure, he finds the supper his mother prepared for him and it is still hot. We imagine the meal on his bed stand is a hot, creamy bowl of macaroni and cheese, and that is precisely what inspired this recipe.

Ingredients

1 box of pasta

4 T. unsalted butter

3 T. all-purpose flour

2 C whole milk, room temperature

1 C sharp yellow cheddar cheese, grated

1 C aged white cheddar cheese, grated

3–4 T. high-quality Parmesan cheese, grated

Salt and pepper to taste

1 C cooked peas, spinach, broccoli, or other favorite green (optional)

> Rotini, cavatappi, shell, and elbow pasta work well for rich sauces.

Directions

1. Bring a large pot of water to a rolling boil. Generously salt the water. Add the pasta and cook according to the instructions. When ready, strain and set aside.

2. While the pasta is cooking, melt the butter in a saucepan on medium heat. Whisk the flour into the butter a few tablespoons at a time. Continue whisking for several minutes until well combined. Add the milk in half-cup portions, whisking throughout to achieve a thick but smooth, sauce-like consistency. Salt and pepper the sauce to taste.

3. Remove from the heat. Add the grated cheeses to the sauce 1 cup or so at a time, and stir until the cheese is melted and the sauce is thick and smooth.

4. Pour the cheese sauce over the pasta and gently stir until the noodles are well dressed. Stir in greens, if using. Serve warm, preferably after a night of great adventure.

The creamiest macaroni and cheese inspired by *Where the Wild Things Are* by Maurice Sendak

A CHANCE OF SPAGHETTI & MEATBALLS

Serves 6+ | Hard | AA | D | G | GF (with gluten-free spaghetti and breadcrumbs) | K | M | O | S

We could write an entire cookbook about *Cloudy with a Chance of Meatballs*, a book about a town where meals rain down like weather, but in the end we chose to do a recipe inspired by the title of the book because spaghetti and meatballs is one of our favorite meals ever. This recipe—one that my family has made for years and years—is not easy, but you can do it. The trick is to read the recipe first and get organized, and then begin.

Ingredients

3 T. olive oil

⅓ C diced onions

⅓ C diced celery

⅓ C diced carrots

3 T. chopped basil

1–2 bay leaves

1 small piece of lemon rind

1½ pounds lean ground beef (85% lean works well)

¼ t. nutmeg

2 eggs

½ C breadcrumbs (you can use gluten-free breadcrumbs if you prefer)

2 T. milk

1 T. mixed dried herbs (a mixture of oregano, rosemary, basil, and parsley work well)

1 C Parmesan cheese, grated and divided in half

1 box of spaghetti (you can use gluten-free spaghetti if you prefer)

2 28-oz. cans whole peeled tomatoes, blended

Salt and pepper to taste

Directions

1. Preheat the oven to 375°F.

2. Heat the olive oil in a large saucepan over medium heat. When the oil is heated through, add the onions, celery, carrots, 1 tablespoon of basil, bay leaves, and lemon rind to the oil. Sauté on medium-high heat until the onions are translucent and the celery and carrots are tender, but not too soft.

3. While the vegetables are sautéing, in a large bowl, combine the ground beef, nutmeg, and a generous amount of salt and pepper.

4. When the vegetables are ready, add about a pound (⅔rds) of the ground beef mixture to the pan with the vegetables. Using a spatula, break up the meat into small pieces. You want it to cook in small crumbles and not in one large piece. Sauté the meat for 10 minutes or so, until just cooked through.

5. While the meat is cooking, in a large bowl, combine the remaining ground beef with the eggs, breadcrumbs, milk, herbs, and half of the Parmesan cheese. Mix with your hands until all ingredients are fully combined. Add salt and pepper to taste. Using your hands, take a pinch of the meat mixture and form into a ball just about the size of a golf ball (no larger). Place the meatball on a baking tray. Repeat until the entire mixture is finished. Bake in the oven for 10 minutes, turning the meatballs over with tongs or a spatula at the 5-minute mark so they cook evenly. When the meatballs are browned around the outside, take them out of the oven (don't worry if they are not cooked through—they will cook further in the sauce).

6. While the meatballs are cooking in the oven, bring a large pot of water to a big, rolling boil. Generously salt the boiling water. Add the spaghetti and cook according to the instructions (err on the side of cooking the pasta slightly less for an authentic, al dente bite!). When ready, strain and set aside.

7. When the sautéed meat and vegetable mixture on the stove has cooked through, add the blended tomatoes and more salt and pepper to taste. Stir until the meat and tomatoes are well combined. Bring the sauce to a simmer and add the baked meatballs. Allow the meat sauce and meatballs to cook on medium heat for 15 to 20 minutes (or as long as a half-hour for a thicker sauce). Turn the meatballs over here and there to be sure they are cooking evenly.

8. When the sauce is nice and thick, take it off the heat. Remove the bay leaves and lemon rind. In a large serving bowl, combine the cooked pasta with the sauce and meatballs and stir gently, being careful not to break the spaghetti or meatballs. Sprinkle with the remaining Parmesan cheese and basil. Serve hot.

> When making tomato sauce, you can place the tomatoes in a blender and blend until smooth, or pour into a large bowl and blend thoroughly with an "immersion" or hand blender.

TENDERLOIN AT THE PLAZA

Serves 4–6 | Hard | Adventurous | AA | GF | K | M | O | S

Eloise—the character and the book—holds a special place in our hearts. We have read this book dozens of times and we still delight in Eloise's adventures at the Plaza Hotel (where Poppy and I made a recent pilgrimage!). We follow her as she rides up and down the elevator and laugh and laugh when she busts out with, "Oh what a love-a-ly mawning." Eloise loves to make mischief and she loves to order room service with Nanny. At breakfast, Nanny eats Irish bacon and at dinnertime, Eloise orders beef tenderloin. We have combined the two for a delicious and fancy meal that is the perfect tribute to Eloise—ooooooooo how we love her!

Ingredients

1 (2¼ lbs.) high-quality beef tenderloin roast

3 T. olive oil

1–2 T. of fresh rosemary, finely chopped

1–2 T. of fresh thyme, finely chopped

Salt and pepper to taste

10–12 strips of high-quality bacon

10 or so toothpicks, soaked in water

> Soaking toothpicks in water before they take heat from a grill or oven ensures they don't catch on fire.

Directions

1. Preheat the oven to 375°F.

2. Place the tenderloin on a large cutting board. Drizzle the olive oil over the tenderloin slowly, using your hands to guide the oil. The olive oil should coat the bottom as well as the top of the loin.

3. In a small bowl, combine the rosemary and thyme and salt and pepper to taste. Sprinkle the herb and seasoning mixture over the meat, making sure the mixture covers the top and bottom. Set aside.

4. Pat down the bacon strips with a paper towel to remove any excess liquid. Lay the bacon down flat one after the other, side by side on a baking tray. Lay the tenderloin in the center of the bacon. Wrap one piece of bacon at a time up and around the tenderloin, making a tight circle with each strip. Using toothpicks, secure the bacon near the top of the loin where the bacon strips meet. Set aside.

5. Heat a large pan (large enough to fit the entire tenderloin length-wise) on medium-high heat. Place the tenderloin in the pan. Cook on medium-high heat for 3 to 5 minutes or until the bacon begins to turn golden. Repeat all the way around, using tongs to carefully turn the tenderloin each time (avoid the side with the toothpicks).

6. Transfer the tenderloin back to the baking tray. Cook in the oven for 20 to 25 minutes, until well done on the outside and medium-pink on the inside.

7. Remove the tenderloin from the oven and let rest for 8 to 10 minutes. Cut into slices of desired thickness and serve warm. Don't forget to remove the toothpicks before serving.

Beef tenderloin wrapped in Irish bacon inspired by *Eloise* by Kay Thompson

MOUNTAIN OF HAMBURGERS

Serves 3–4 | Medium | AA | D (with cheese) | G | GF (with gluten-free buns) | M | N(O) | S

I Love You, Stinky Face is a sweet book about how much mamas love their children. The mama in the book would love her little boy even if he turned into a smelly skunk or a terrible meat-eating dinosaur. In fact, she would make that meat-eating dinosaur a mountain of hamburgers to eat—juicy hamburgers just like our recipe below! Top these burgers with anything your heart desires and enjoy with your mama. After all, she loves you the most!

Ingredients

1 pound of 85% lean ground beef

Salt and pepper to taste

Any of your favorite toppings, including cheese, lettuce, tomato, onion, pickle, avocado, ketchup, mustard, and anything else you like

High-quality hamburger buns or a bun alternative, like whole wheat toast or French baguette (you can use gluten-free buns if you prefer)

Directions

1. Heat a large pan (or grill, if it's warm out) to medium-high heat. Place the ground beef in a large bowl and add a generous amount of salt and pepper. Mix the ground beef with your hands until the salt and pepper are well incorporated.

2. Using your hands, form 3 large- or 4 medium-sized patties. Flatten the patties down quite a bit—they will retract with the heat.

3. Cook the patties in the pan to your desired temperature, flipping halfway through. In the last 2 to 3 minutes of cooking, top with cheese, if using, and cover with a lid so the cheese melts.

4. Take your patties off the heat, assemble on buns with your choice of toppings, and serve!

Our favorite toppings for burgers are mashed avocado, almond slivers, a rich cheese called Saint-André, and a touch of honey!

Juicy, messy hamburgers inspired by *I Love You, Stinky Face* by Lisa McCourt

A FEAST OF STONES SOUP

Serves 3–4 | Medium | AA | D | G | GF (if using brown rice; barley does contain gluten) | K | S | V | VE (with non-dairy milk)

In *Stone Soup*, three soldiers trick a village of people into giving them ingredients to make a hearty and indulgent soup. The soldiers start the soup with only water and stones, and they manage to get more and more ingredients as they go. Our rendition of stone soup is rock-free, but it is just as hearty and filling as the soup in the book. While we didn't trick anyone into helping us make it, we do think it is best enjoyed with your village, whoever that might be.

Ingredients

1 C barley or brown rice

3 T. olive oil

½ large yellow onion, diced

2 celery stalks, diced

2 carrots, diced

2–3 t. dried rosemary, crushed in your palm to release flavor

32 oz. high-quality homemade or store-bought vegetable broth.

1 can garbanzo beans, drained and rinsed

1 can cannellini beans, drained and rinsed

1 can pinto beans, drained and rinsed

1 C whole milk (not all milk substitutes will work here and you may have to experiment—the milk substitute should be thick and creamy, like a coconut milk)

Salt and pepper to taste

Directions

1. In a medium pot, cook barley or brown rice according to the instructions on the package.

2. In the meantime, heat the olive oil in a large saucepot over medium heat. Add the onions, celery, carrots, and rosemary to the oil. Sauté on medium heat until the onions are translucent and the celery and carrots are tender but not too soft.

3. Next, add the vegetable broth to the pan and bring to a boil, adjusting the heat as necessary. Once the broth boils, reduce to a simmer for 2 to 3 minutes. Then, gently stir in the beans and milk and bring the soup back up to a simmer.

4. Using an "immersion" or hand blender, blend the soup just slightly to create a smooth, creamy texture. (Alternatively, if you don't have a hand blender, scoop 2 cups of the soup with a ladle and place in a blender. Let the soup cool in the blender uncovered for several minutes before blending. Do not blend right away. The liquid will be too hot and the heat can cause the contents to spill out. When you do blend, blend on low and cover the lid with a towel.) Finally, stir in the barley or rice, and add salt and pepper to taste.

5. Serve piping hot in heaping spoonfuls with a side of crusty buttered bread.

I typically keep about 20 ounces of vegetable broth by the stove as I make this recipe, with an additional 10 or so in the refrigerator or pantry as back up. Once you've added the beans, if you prefer the soup to be more "brothy," you can add some additional liquid as desired.

Hearty, indulgent mixed bean soup inspired by
Stone Soup by Marcia Brown

DRAGON TACOS

Serves 4–6 | **Hard** | Adventurous | AA | D | GF | K | M | S

This book is hilarious—random and funny and "on trend" since tacos are all the rage these days! The dragons in the book love tacos, but not spicy ones. Lots of problems ensue when they eat spicy tacos by accident. This is a lot like taco night at our house, so we cooked up a recipe for tacos even dragons would enjoy. If you are feeling adventurous (and you're not afraid of fire-breathing dragons), you can add the optional hints of spice below.

Ingredients

3 T. olive oil

½ onion, finely chopped

2 garlic cloves, whole

½ green bell pepper, diced

½ jalapeño, diced (optional)

4 oz. can mild green chilies, drained

1½ T. cumin powder

2 T. chili powder (optional)

2 C of pulled, roasted chicken breast

⅓ C chicken broth

2 T. lime juice

½ C cilantro, roughly chopped, plus more for garnish (optional)

Salt and pepper to taste

10–12 corn tortillas

Sour cream (optional)

1 C sharp cheddar cheese, shredded

The seeds are largely where the spice of any pepper comes from; depending on the desired heat, include or discard the seeds.

Directions

1. In a large pan, heat the olive oil over medium heat. When the oil is heated through, add the onion and garlic. Sauté for 5 minutes or so, until the onion softens and becomes translucent. Add the green bell pepper and jalapeño, if using, and continue sautéing, another 5 minutes or so. Next, add the green chilies, cumin, and chili powder, if using. Stir gently until all of the ingredients are well incorporated.

2. Add the chicken and broth to the pan. Stir until the chicken is well incorporated and the broth absorbs slightly, 5 minutes or so.

3. Take the chicken mixture off the heat. Stir in the lime juice and cilantro. Add salt and pepper to taste. Set aside.

4. Place the tortillas on a microwave-safe plate. Lightly dampen several large paper towels with water and tightly wrap the tortillas. Microwave on high for 15 to 20 seconds, until the tortillas are warmed through.

5. Scoop spoonfuls of the chicken mixture into the tortillas. Garnish each with sour cream, if using, plus shredded cheddar and a pinch of cilantro for garnish. Serve and enjoy.

For any recipe that calls for pulled chicken, you can roast the chicken at home the day before, or buy a high-quality whole roasted chicken from a local grocery store and use the skinless breast meat.

Juicy chicken tacos inspired by

Dragons Love Tacos by Adam Rubin

LION AND BIRD GNOCCHI

Serves 4–6 | Hard | Adventurous | AA | D | G | K | N(O) | S | V

A sweet lion rescues a bird when he is injured and cold. They become the closest of friends all through the winter, sitting by a cozy fire and sleeping next to one another in warm beds. In spring, the bird migrates on, and our hearts break wondering what will happen next. These belly filling, piping hot gnocchi are a tribute to the lion and the bird. They are rich and delicious and just the perfect meal for two unlikely friends who come to love each other very much. This recipe is easier than it looks, and you will be so pleased with the result: a special homemade pasta to share with the ones you love.

Ingredients (for Gnocchi)

4–5 Yukon Gold potatoes

1 egg yolk, beaten

All-purpose flour (you will need lots of it—just keep the bag out)

Ingredients (for Pesto)

2 C fresh basil

½ C Parmesan cheese, plus more for sprinkling on top

⅓ C pine nuts (optional)

1 garlic clove (optional)

½ C olive oil, plus a drizzle more (if needed)

2–3 T. vegetable stock (if needed)

Directions (for Gnocchi)

1. Boil a large pot of water. In the meantime, wash the skin of the potatoes thoroughly. Boil the potatoes in the pot of water until tender—you should be able to easily insert a fork all the way through. Set aside until the potatoes are cool enough to handle. (This would be a good time to make the pesto sauce, using the directions on the next page.)

2. Next, gently peel the skin off of the potatoes. Pass the potatoes through a potato ricer and into a large bowl. (If you don't have a potato ricer, mash the potatoes thoroughly with a fork. If you aren't able to get all the lumps out with the fork, spread the mashed potatoes out on a large cutting board with a layer of parchment paper on top. Roll a rolling pin over the potatoes until they are smooth.)

3. Add the egg yolk and a cup or so of flour to the bowl with the potatoes. Using your hands, mix the contents of the bowl well. Next, with one hand in a cupping shape, slowly incorporate more flour into the potato mixture in a circular motion from the bottom up as if you are making a bread dough. Add additional flour as needed one cup at a time and continue incorporating until the mixture easily forms into one big ball and is not sticky. You will use about 4 to 5 cups of flour.

4. Heavily flour a large cutting board. Taking small handful-sized pieces of dough at a time, roll the dough out on the cutting board into long ropes (or snakes), approximately ¾ of an inch around. Continue until the entire dough is formed into long ropes.

5. Using a sharp, thin knife (like a steak knife), cut the ropes into ½ inch squares, or pillows. Continue until you have cut out all of the gnocchi. As you cut out the gnocchi, move them gently to the side of the cutting board. Sprinkle additional flour on the gnocchi as needed so they don't stick together. Set aside.

6. Heat a large pot of water on the stove until it comes to a boil. Salt the water generously. Using a slotted spoon, gently drop the gnocchi 10 or so at a time in to the slow-boiling water until you have dropped them all in. Stir gently once or twice to be sure the gnocchi are not sticking together or to the bottom of the pot. The gnocchi are done when they float to the top of the boiling water, approximately 3 to 4 minutes. Using a slotted spoon, remove the gnocchi

from the water by skimming them off the top in rounds as they are ready and placing them in a large serving bowl.

Directions (for Pesto)

1. While the boiled potatoes are cooling, add the basil and Parmesan cheese (and pine nuts and garlic, if using) to a food processor. Start the processor and slowly drizzle in the olive oil. The pesto should form a thick, sauce-like consistency. If the pesto is not blending easily, add another drizzle of olive oil (or, for a lighter version, you can add a couple tablespoons of vegetable stock instead). Add salt and pepper to taste.

2. Add the pesto to the cooked gnocchi and gently toss until the gnocchi are well coated. Serve with a generous helping of Parmesan cheese sprinkled on top.

Pillowy potato pasta with pesto sauce inspired by *The Lion and the Bird* by Marianne Dubuc

ONE FISH, TWO FISH

Serves 3 | Medium | Adventurous | AA | GF | O

This is a book about all kinds of quirky fish (and devolves into a book about other strange and quirky animals, the way only Dr. Seuss can make happen). Since it's right there in the title, we thought it would be fun to create two different fish recipes, and let you decide which one you like best. Both recipes feature salmon, a meaty fish that, if prepared correctly, is rich, buttery, and completely delicious.

Ingredients

2–3 high-quality salmon filets, deboned with skin on

Salt and pepper to taste

3–4 T. oil (olive oil and grape seed oil are both excellent for this recipe)

½ lemon, sliced into wedges

Directions (Fish Preparation 1)

1. Place the salmon skin-side down on a plastic cutting board. Dry the salmon thoroughly with a paper towel. Salt and pepper both sides generously.

2. Heat a large sauté pan on medium-high heat. Add the oil and heat until the oil glistens, 3 to 4 minutes. Gently place the salmon in the pan. Sear the salmon skin-side down until the edges turn golden brown (approximately 4 to 5 minutes). Turn the salmon over and finish cooking, another few minutes. The edges will be golden and crispy, and the inside will be lightly pink. Serve with lemon wedges for squeezing on top.

Directions (Fish Preparation 2)

1. Preheat the oven to 375°F. Drizzle about ⅓ of the oil directly onto the baking tray and place the tray in the oven for 5 minutes or so to heat the oil. Take the baking tray out of the oven.

2. Carefully place the salmon filets on the heated baking tray skin-side down. Using a spoon, coat the filets with the remaining oil and salt and pepper to taste. Cook in the oven for 15 to 20 minutes, until the filets take on a light pink color and begin to flake. Serve with lemon wedges for squeezing on top.

> Avoid wood cutting boards for fish because the smell has a tendency to settle in.

Two simple but satisfying salmon preparations
inspired by *One Fish, Two Fish, Red Fish, Blue Fish*
by Dr. Seuss

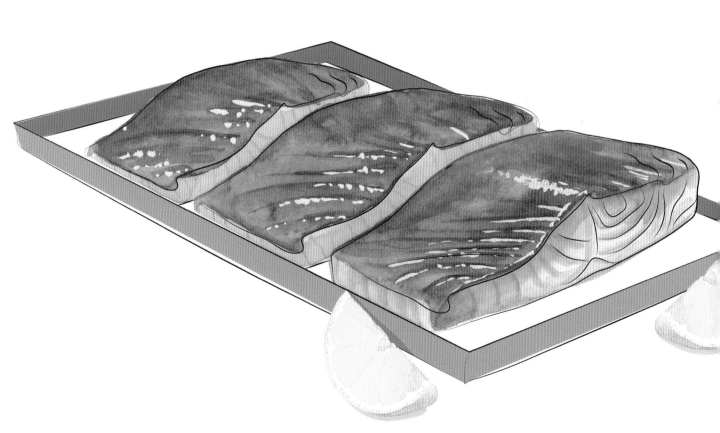

VEGGIE, SALAD, & SIDE RECIPES

THE CREEPIEST CARROTS

Serves 4–6 | Medium | AA | GF | O | V | VE

Johnny was born on Halloween, so we appreciate anything with a spooky or creepy vibe. And lately, *Creepy Carrots!* has become one of Jude's favorites, too. This funny book about carrots who follow a little rabbit around town makes the perfect inspiration for roasted carrots, which turn crispy and toasty and a little twisty in the oven, looking a whole lot like the creepy carrots in the book. Don't fear, though! They taste delicious.

Ingredients

1 large bundle of carrots (heirloom or organic are a good option), washed and with tops trimmed

½ C olive oil

⅓ C fresh parsley, roughly chopped (optional)

Sea salt to taste

Directions

1. Preheat the oven to medium broil (if you don't have a broil setting on your oven, preheat the oven to 425°F). Line the carrots on a baking dish or tray. Coat thoroughly in olive oil.

2. Broil on a middle rack for 20 to 25 minutes, until the skins begin to brown and wrinkle (creepy!) and the carrots are tender all the way through. Check on the carrots at the 10-minute mark to make sure they are cooking nicely and that the oven isn't too hot. Using a wooden spoon or spatula, turn the carrots here and there to expose them to the broiler uniformly. If the carrots are getting too brown, reduce the broil temperature to low.

3. When ready, take the carrots out of the oven. Sprinkle with parsley, if using, and sea salt. Serve warm.

For some recipes, cutting ingredients uniformly is important so that the ingredients cook evenly. For this recipe, you can cut the larger carrots in half length-wise so the carrots are all uniform in thickness.

Warm roasted carrots inspired by *Creepy Carrots!* by Aaron Reynolds

HAROLD'S BEETS

Serves 4–6 | Easy | Adventurous | AA | D | GF | K | N(O) | V

Harold takes off around the world with a purple crayon, and he proudly colors his entire world purple. Nothing gives off a more beautiful purple hue than beets, and they are the most naturally sweet vegetable we can think of. This salad, with a little sweetness from the beets, a little tartness from the orange, some richness from the goat cheese, and, most importantly, the deep purple color, is just the kind of thing Harold would color for himself.

Ingredients

1 orange

5–6 ready-to-eat beets (you can find these in the produce department of most grocery stores), diced into bite-sized, uniform pieces

⅓ C pistachios

⅓ C high-quality olive oil

Salt and pepper to taste

½ C crumbled goat cheese

3–4 mint leaves, roughly chopped (optional)

Directions

1. Cut the top and bottom off of the orange. Using a sharp knife, cut along the edge of the orange in a downward motion from top to bottom to remove the peel and pith (white part of the skin). The best way to do this is to make an almost C shape down the orange as you are cutting the peel. Next, using the same knife, cut in between the natural white segment lines of the orange until you have slices with no skin on either side (this is called "supreming"). Once you have extracted the segments, set the remaining orange pulp aside.

2. Place the beets, orange slices, and pistachios in a large salad bowl. Set aside.

3. In a medium bowl, whisk together olive oil, salt, and pepper. Squeeze the leftover orange pulp into the olive oil and whisk further, until the olive oil and orange dressing are well combined. Pour the dressing into the salad bowl and stir gently until all of the ingredients are well coated in the dressing.

4. Sprinkle goat cheese and mint leaves on top, if using. Serve at room temperature.

Bright and earthy purple beets inspired by *Harold and the Purple Crayon* by Crockett Johnson

SECRET GARDEN GREENS

Serves 4–6 | Easy | Adventurous | AA | D | GF | K | V

We have been reading *The Secret Garden* since the kids were very small. We love the quiet of the garden and the friends who bring it to life. This delicious, bright garden salad is full of things that we imagine are growing behind the secret garden walls—wholesome, fresh, delicious ingredients that nurture us to health.

Ingredients

1 head Boston or butter lettuce, washed, dried, and roughly cut (you can use your hands to pull the lettuce apart)

1 C frozen green peas, brought to room temperature

2 T. chives, finely chopped

⅓ C avocado, mashed until smooth

⅓ C plain whole milk yogurt

½ C olive oil

⅓ C freshly squeezed lemon juice

⅓ C raw sunflower seeds

Salt and pepper to taste

Directions

1. Place the lettuce, peas, and chives in a large salad bowl. Set aside.

2. In a medium bowl, combine avocado, yogurt, olive oil, and lemon juice. Using a whisk, whisk the ingredients vigorously until well combined. The consistency will be a thick, smooth dressing. Pour the dressing slowly over the salad until it is as dressed as you like it. Toss to combine. Sprinkle with sunflower seeds, if using, and salt and pepper to taste.

3. Serve as a light lunch or a side dish at dinnertime.

A bright, fresh salad inspired by *The Secret Garden* by Frances Hodgson Burnett

TERRIBLE, HORRIBLE, NO GOOD, VERY BAD GREENS

Serves 3–4 | Medium | Adventurous | AA | GF | K | O | V | VE

Alexander is having a terrible, horrible, no good, very bad day. We can certainly relate to that! On this terrible, horrible, no good, very bad day, he absolutely refuses to eat lima beans. We can relate to that too! This recipe is our solution to both; it is the perfect, kid-friendly way to cook any and all greens and green vegetables. The greens turn out crispy, a little salty, and delicious every time. This recipe reminds us how much we actually love vegetables, and eating healthful greens with high-quality olive oil make us feel good inside too.

Ingredients

3–4 C or 1–2 stalks of thoroughly washed greens, including one or more of the following: asparagus, broccoli, Brussels sprouts, cauliflower, green beans, or lima beans (all are on rotation at our house and work well with this recipe)

⅓ C high-quality olive oil

Salt and pepper to taste

Directions

1. Preheat the oven to 425°F.

2. Place the greens on a baking sheet or baking dish. If you are using long thin greens, like asparagus or green beans, leave them whole. If you are using thicker, denser greens, like broccoli or Brussels sprouts, cut them in half or quarters depending on the thickness of the bunch. Coat thoroughly with olive oil. Add salt and pepper to taste.

3. Bake for 15 to 25 minutes depending on the desired texture. We prefer ours cooked slightly longer, so they have a golden brown coating and a little crispiness to the edges. When the greens are ready, take them out of the oven. Serve warm.

The most delicious green vegetables inspired by Alexander and the Terrible, Horrible, No Good, Very Bad Day by Judith Viorst

ONE POTATO, TWO POTATO

Oven Roasted | Serves 6 | Medium | AA | GF | K | O | V | VE
Smashed | Serves 6 | Medium | AA | D | GF | S | V

In *One Potato, Two Potato*, Mr. and Mrs. O'Grady have one of everything to share until they find a magic pot that doubles everything. Naturally then, we were inspired to create two different potato dishes depending on what we are in the mood for. The first recipe makes crispy, oven-roasted fries that are just addictive. The second is our favorite, super simple mashed potato recipe that is as perfect for a weeknight meal as it is for an indulgent holiday spread.

Ingredients (Roasted)

6 medium potatoes, any variety

¼ C high-quality olive oil, plus a drizzle for the sheet pan

3–4 sprigs fresh rosemary, removed from the stem

1–2 T. Herbs de Provence

Salt and pepper to taste

Ingredients (Smashed)

6 red potatoes

¼ C high-quality olive oil

½ C sour cream

½ C milk

1 T. Herbs de Provence

Salt and pepper to taste

¼ C Parmesan cheese

Directions (Roasted)

1. Preheat the oven to 450°F.

2. Wash the potatoes thoroughly and cut them into thick, French fry-like shapes. Place the cut potatoes in a large bowl. Toss the potatoes with olive oil, rosemary, herbs, and salt and pepper until the potatoes are well coated. Set aside.

3. Drizzle olive oil onto a large, rimmed baking sheet and tilt the sheet back and forth to distribute the oil across the pan. Place the baking sheet in the oven for 3 to 5 minutes to heat up the oil. Remove the baking sheet from the oven.

4. Carefully place the potatoes on the baking sheet. Return the baking sheet to the oven and bake for 30 minutes, or until the edges of the potatoes begin to get crispy and brown. Stir the potatoes halfway through to be sure they are cooking evenly. Serve hot.

Directions (Smashed)

1. Wash the potatoes thoroughly. Fill a large pot with cool water. Place the potatoes in the pot of cool water and put on the stove. Turn the heat to high and cover partially with a lid. When the water reaches a rolling boil, reduce to a slow boil and cook until the potatoes are fork tender all the way through.

2. Drain the potatoes and transfer them to a large, heat-safe bowl. Add the remaining ingredients except the Parmesan cheese to the bowl. Using

the back of a fork or a potato masher, mash the potatoes to the desired consistency. Alternate mashing the potatoes and stirring once or twice around to ensure the added ingredients are being fully incorporated into the potatoes. Add the Parmesan cheese and stir once or twice more to incorporate. Serve immediately.

Crispy fries and mashed potatoes inspired by *One Potato, Two Potato* by Cynthia DeFelice

DESSERT RECIPES

HUNNY CAKE

Serves 1–2 | Easy | AA | D | GF | N | V

Winnie the Pooh is a sweet and thoughtful little bear who lives in the Hundred Acre Wood, where he goes on many adventures with his friends Piglet and Eeyore and Owl and Christopher Robin and others. This quick and easy honey cake is a tribute to Pooh's favorite food, "hunny," and the warm gooey cake will make you feel like a plump little stuffed bear. This cake is microwave only, so kiddos can handle this recipe almost entirely themselves.

Ingredients

2 T. coconut flour

2 T. almond flour

⅛ t. salt

1 t. pumpkin pie spice (if you don't have pumpkin pie spice, cinnamon will do)

½ t. baking powder

1 T. honey

½ T. maple syrup

½ t. high-quality vanilla extract

1 egg white

⅓ C milk

1 T. mashed banana

A handful of white chocolate chips for sprinkling

Directions

1. In a small bowl, combine the flours, salt, pumpkin pie spice, and baking powder. Set aside.

2. In a separate small bowl, whisk together the honey, maple syrup, vanilla, egg white, milk, and banana. Pour the wet ingredients over the dry ingredients and stir until just combined.

3. Pour the batter into a tall, microwave-safe mug. Microwave on high for 1½ to 2 minutes, or until the batter begins to rise up in the mug. Watch the batter as it is cooking to be sure it doesn't spill over the edge.

4. Take the mug out of the microwave and let the cake cool for a minute or so. Sprinkle with white chocolate chips and serve directly in the mug (or scoop out half to share with a friend)!

A sweet and simple honey mug cake inspired by *Winnie the Pooh* by A. A. Milne

IF YOU GIVE A KID A COOKIE, COOKIES

Makes 10–12 large to medium squares | Medium | AA | D | G | O | V

If You Give a Mouse a Cookie is a children's classic. According to the book, if you give a mouse a cookie, he will ask you for some milk, and then the asking never ends. As it turns out, if you give a kiddo a decadent, pan chocolate chip cookie, they'll ask you for some milk, and some more cookies, and well...let's just say it's a lot like when you give a mouse a cookie!

Ingredients

2 C all-purpose flour

¼ C whole wheat flour

1 t. baking soda

1 t. kosher salt

1 C unsalted butter, softened

½ C sugar

1 C brown sugar

2 eggs

1 t. vanilla

1 t. almond extract

1½ C bittersweet chocolate chunks or chips

Directions

1. Preheat the oven to 375°F.

2. Generously grease a 9×13-inch baking dish with the butter wrapper. Set aside.

3. In a large bowl, combine the flours, baking soda, and salt. Set aside.

4. Using a handheld or stand mixer, beat the butter and sugars until well combined and fluffy. Add the eggs, vanilla, and almond extract and beat further, until well combined. Slowly add the flour mixture to the butter mixture and beat further, until well combined. Using a spatula or wooden spoon, fold in the chocolate chunks or chips.

5. Scoop the batter into the baking dish and spread into an even layer. Bake for 15 to 20 minutes, or until a toothpick inserted in the center comes out clean.

6. Cool on a cooling rack. Cut into squares and serve at your own risk!

Rich and gooey chocolate chip cookies inspired by
If You Give a Mouse a Cookie by Laura Numeroff

BROWN BEAR BROWNIES

Makes 9 or 12 squares | Medium | AA | D | G | O | V

At the start of this book, I said that my love of brownies came from a cookbook I had as a child. To this day, brownies are my favorite dessert, and one of my favorite treats to make for my family. This recipe in particular, which we have worked on for years now, makes chewy, rich brownies, and the brownies look quite a bit like the bear on the cover of *Brown Bear, Brown Bear, What Do You See?*, one of our all-time favorite books that we have been reading since the day the kids were born.

Ingredients

½ C all-purpose flour

1 C sugar

⅓ C unsweetened cocoa powder

¼ t. salt

½ C unsalted butter, melted, plus more
for greasing the pan

2 eggs

1 t. vanilla

1–2 t. powdered sugar for dusting (optional)

Directions

1. Preheat the oven to 350°F. Grease an 8x8-inch baking pan with butter.

2. In a medium bowl, sift the flour, sugar, cocoa powder, and salt. In another small bowl, whisk together the butter, eggs, and vanilla. Add the egg mixture into the flour mixture, stirring until just combined. Pour the mixture into the greased pan.

3. Bake for 30 to 35 minutes, or until a toothpick inserted in the center comes out clean. Remove from the oven and let cool for 5 minutes. Cut into squares, dust with powdered sugar if using, and serve.

Decadent brownies inspired by *Brown Bear, Brown Bear, What Do You See?* by Bill Martin Jr. and Eric Carle

ALL THE CRAYONS FRUIT SALAD

Serves 4–6 | Easy | AA | GF | K | V | VE

The Day the Crayons Quit is a book about a bunch of whiny crayons. Red needs a rest. Purple is outside the lines. Black wants a beach ball. Orange and yellow can't agree...and so on. In the end, though, they come together to create a beautiful picture. This fruit salad, a lovely harmony of all different kinds of fruits in all different kinds of big, bold colors, is our best interpretation of the crayons coming together, and of how beautiful things are when we find ways to get along.

Ingredients

Choose a colorful assortment of your favorite in-season fruit, including:

10 or so strawberries, cut into bite-sized pieces

1 apple, cut into bite-sized pieces

1 peach, sliced

1 nectarine, cut into bite-sized pieces

2 kiwis, cut into bite-sized pieces

10–20 blueberries

10–20 grapes, cut in half

1 banana, sliced

4–5 mint leaves, torn by hand

Directions

1. In a large bowl, combine all of the fruit except the banana. Gently toss the fruit until it is well combined, being careful not to break the fruit.

2. Arrange the banana slices in a circle around the edge of the bowl. Sprinkle mint leaves over the entire dish. Serve chilled or at room temperature.

A salad of all of your favorite fruit inspired by
The Day the Crayons Quit by Drew Daywalt

COZY CORDUROY COOKIES

Makes 14 to 16 cookies | Medium | AA | D | G | O | V

Corduroy is all about the warmth and coziness of a loving home, and nothing says home to us like these soft, buttery, melt-in-your-mouth cookies, which, much like Corduroy's little button, have a tendency to go missing as soon as they're baked! These cookies are great for sharing with friends or eating with your family as a dessert or special midnight snack, and will make you feel safe and protected like you are being wrapped up in the arms of the people who love you most.

Ingredients

1 C unsalted butter, softened

1 C powdered sugar

¾ C granulated sugar

1 large egg

1½ t. high-quality vanilla extract

½ t. salt

½ t. baking powder

1½ C all-purpose flour, sifted

Directions

1. In a large mixing bowl using an electric mixer, beat the butter and sugars until they are creamy and smooth. Beat in the egg, vanilla, salt, and baking powder. Using a spatula, stir in the flour until the mixture forms a dough. With your hands, shape the dough into 3 evenly sized flat disks about 1 to 2 inches thick. Cover the disks with parchment paper and chill for an hour or so.

2. Preheat the oven to 350°F.

3. Roll the dough out on a cutting board or parchment paper to about ⅓-inch thickness. Using the rim of a small glass or circle-shaped cookie cutter, cut the dough into circles. Mush the scraps of leftover dough back together, roll out again, and make more circles until you've used all of the dough.

4. Bake the cookies in the oven for 8 to 10 minutes, until the edges are a light golden color. Cool on a cooling rack completely (or for as long as you can wait!).

Soft, buttery sugar cookies inspired by *Corduroy*
by Don Freeman

CHARLIE'S CHOCOLATE PUDDING

Serves 3–4 | Easy | Adventurous | AA | D | GF | V | VE (with non-dairy milk)

The story of *Charlie and the Chocolate Factory* by one of our favorite children's authors, Roald Dahl, is a whimsical delight. It is the ultimate childhood fantasy, with mystery and intrigue and sweets at every turn. This chia seed pudding embodies that, with a rich depth of flavors in the chocolate-maple pudding, the great texture of the chia seeds, and the hint of spicy cinnamon. This dish is also good for you, full of super foods and healthy sources of sweetness. We like it with homemade, unsweetened whipped cream, coconut flakes, and fruit on top, but feel free to top it with any whimsical toppings you like!

Ingredients

2 C milk

½ t. high-quality vanilla extract

2 T. maple syrup

¼ t. cinnamon

¼ C unsweetened cocoa powder

½–¾ C chia seeds (the more chia seeds you use, the thicker the pudding)

Directions

1. Whisk all ingredients except the chia seeds together until well incorporated. Whisk in the chia seeds. Pour the mixture into a jar or glass container and place in the refrigerator for at least 4 hours or, preferably, overnight. Eat cold out of the refrigerator with toppings of your choice.

Rich chocolate chia seed pudding inspired by *Charlie and the Chocolate Factory* by Roald Dahl

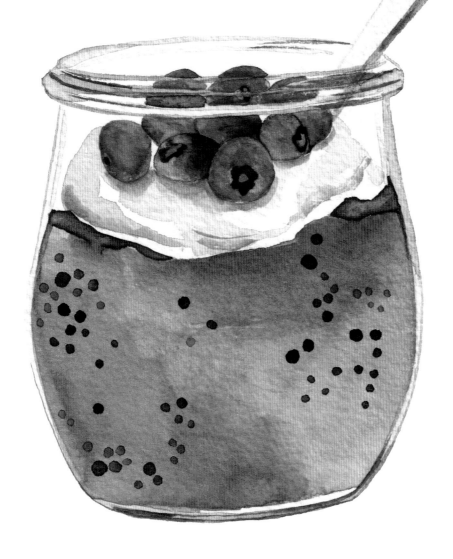

PEACH DREAMS

Serves 3–4 | Medium | AA | GF | K | V | VE

In *James and the Giant Peach*, a little boy with some wicked aunts finds himself in the center of a giant peach floating in the ocean. He's got to learn how to get by and get along with the other bugs and creatures who are also in the peach. Early on, he bites into the juicy flesh of the peach and we can't help but imagine the burst of peach flavor that he gulps down. This recipe is a tribute to that—a rich but healthful banana-based ice cream, bursting with peach flavor. Because this ice cream is mostly banana and peach, it doesn't hold up too well in the freezer long-term. We recommend eating it all in one sitting, like we do!

Ingredients

3 bananas

½ peach, cut into rough chunks

2–3 T. coconut cream, skimmed off the top of a can of coconut milk

1 whole vanilla bean

Healthy peach ice cream inspired by *James and the Giant Peach* by Roald Dahl

Directions

1. Cut the bananas into small pieces and freeze until solid, at least 2 hours.

2. Ten to 15 minutes before the bananas are ready, blend the peach chunks until smooth. Place in a freezer-safe container and transfer to the freezer to chill.

3. In the meantime, split open the vanilla bean long ways with a thin, sharp knife. Using the back of the knife or a small spoon, scoop out the vanilla bean seeds (or vanilla "caviar") from the inside of the bean. Place the seeds in a small bowl and set aside.

4. When the bananas are ready, place them in the blender and blend until smooth and creamy. Stop the blender periodically and, using a spatula, scrape down the sides as needed to encourage the mixture to blend smoothly. Add the coconut cream one tablespoon at a time to encourage the mixture further. Once the banana mixture is smooth, add the peach puree and vanilla bean seeds. Pulse quickly to incorporate.

5. Serve immediately.

TART WAS ONCE AN APPLE PIE

Serves 8–10 | Medium | AA | D | G | K | O | V

"A" *Was Once an Apple Pie*, as was this tart! In the book, the letters of the alphabet each stand for something, followed by a nonsensical rhyme. We think it's hilarious, especially if read in a singsong way. This recipe is equally funny, in that what was supposed to be an apple pie somehow became an apple tart over time, but we love this recipe anyway. It's easy to pull together with ingredients you have around the house, and there's nothing better than eating it warm out of the oven with a dollop of ice cream on top.

Ingredients

2½ C all-purpose flour

3 T sugar

1 t. salt

1½ sticks chilled butter, plus 2 T. for the filling

¼ C yogurt

⅓ C ice water

2–3 large Granny Smith apples, cut into ½ inch cubes (Granny Smith apples are best to use in this recipe as they stay firm and hold together when cooked)

½ C honey

¼ C fresh squeezed lemon juice

1 T. cinnamon

Directions

1. In a food processor, combine the flour, sugar, salt, and butter. Pulse until the mixture is crumbly. Add the yogurt and pulse further, another 5 seconds or so.

2. Place the dough on a piece of plastic wrap and flatten a bit (it will still be crumbly at this point). Add the water a drizzle at a time and knead until the dough comes together. Form into a disk, wrap in plastic, and refrigerate for an hour or more.

3. In the meantime, in a large bowl, combine the apples, honey, lemon, and cinnamon.

4. When the dough is ready, preheat the oven to 375°F. Roll the dough out in a large, flat circle onto a silicone baking mat or a parchment-lined baking sheet. Put the apple mixture in the middle of the dough and fold up the sides of the tart around the apples, leaving the center of the tart uncovered. Cut the remaining butter into small pieces and place on top of the apples.

5. Bake for 30 to 35 minutes, or until the crust is golden. Serve warm with ice cream on top.

An easy apple tart recipe inspired by "A" *Was Once an Apple Pie* by Edward Lear

SUMMER FAIR CARROT CAKE

Serves 10–12 | Medium | AA | D | G | O | V

Poppy and I adore this sweet book about superfairies who help animal friends in need in a magical little place called Peaseblossom Woods. There is a story for every season, and each season brings delicious and comforting food to go with it. In one of our favorite stories, the rabbits in Rabbit Ridge are preparing a carrot cake for the summer fair. Since carrot cake is a beloved dessert in our house (and one we make on Abe's birthday), we knew we wanted to include it here. This recipe was passed down from my mom who has been making it for ages. We love the natural sweetness from the pineapple and the texture of the grated carrots. Top with cream cheese frosting for a treat that is as delightful as the superfairies themselves!

Ingredients (for Cake)

1½ C all-purpose flour

1 C sugar

1 t. cinnamon

1 t. baking powder

1 t. baking soda

2 eggs

⅔ C vegetable oil

3 medium carrots, grated (about two cups)

1 C canned pineapple (no sugar added), drained

1 t. vanilla

Ingredients (for Frosting)

½ C butter, room temperature

8 oz. cream cheese, room temperature

1 t. vanilla

2 C powdered sugar (you can use more or less powdered sugar depending on how sweet you want the frosting to be)

2–3 T. carrot shavings, optional

Directions (for Cake)

1. Preheat the oven to 350°F.

2. In a large bowl, combine the flour, sugar, cinnamon, baking powder, and baking soda. Mix well. Set aside.

3. In a separate large bowl, whisk together the eggs and oil. Stir in the carrots, pineapple, and vanilla until well combined. Add the dry ingredients to the wet ingredients and mix well.

4. Generously grease a Bundt pan with cooking spray. Pour the batter into the pan. Bake for 50 to 55 minutes, or until a toothpick inserted in the center comes out clean. Turn the cake out of the Bundt pan and let cool completely on a cooling rack.

Directions (for Frosting)

1. Using a handheld or stand mixer, mix together the butter, cream cheese, and vanilla until smooth. Add the powdered sugar slowly until it reaches the right sweetness and consistency, to taste. Decorate the carrot cake (once cooled) with the frosting and carrot shavings, if using, and serve.

A sweet and light carrot cake inspired by *Superfairies: Adventures in Peaseblossom Woods* by Janey Louise Jones

BEVERAGE RECIPES

CHICKA CHICKA BOOM BLISS

Serves 1–2 | Easy | AA | GF | N | V | VE

We have read the book *Chicka Chicka Boom Boom* so many times, we know it by heart. In fact, we spent an entire afternoon once swinging on the swings while reciting the words over and over again. "A told B and B told C, 'I'll meet you at the top of the coconut tree.'" Speaking of coconut trees, this book inspired us to create a coconut-based recipe. What we came up with is a sweet, healthy, and delicious drink that you can make for breakfast, an afternoon snack, or anytime you're on the go!

Ingredients

2 C coconut water

2 T. almond butter

1 banana

Handful of ice

Directions

1. Add all of the ingredients to a blender. Blend until smooth. Enjoy!

A blissful coconut drink inspired by *Chicka Chicka Boom Boom* by Bill Martin Jr. and John Archambault

KITTEN SMOOTHIE

Serves 2–3 | Medium | AA | D | GF | V

This colorful and healthful smoothie was borne from the pages of *The Color Kittens*, where two kittens with bright green eyes splash buckets of paint, one color into another. Our smoothie does the same. With blue and purple berries, bright green spinach, and swirls of apple, yogurt, and orange, we are combining all kinds of colors into one, and the result is a bright fruit smoothie that is as healthy as it is delicious.

Ingredients

2 C mixed frozen berries

Handful of spinach

¼ C hot herbal tea of your choice,
steeped 3–4 minutes

2–3 T. high-quality, sugar-free applesauce

2–3 T. plain yogurt

¼ C freshly squeezed orange juice

1–2 t. honey (optional)

Directions

1. Combine all of the ingredients in a blender. Blend until smooth. If the smoothie is too frozen to blend thoroughly, add an additional tablespoon or so of tea at a time until it blends easily. Serve immediately.

Adding tea to smoothies gives the smoothie a nice, sweet flavor and melts the frozen fruit a bit so it's easier to blend.

A frozen fruit smoothie inspired by *The Color Kittens* by Margaret Wise Brown

STAR WARS WATER

Makes many assorted drinks | Easy | AA | GF | K | V | VE

In recent years, *Star Wars* has become one of our favorite stories, with all sorts of Star Wars books holding court on various bookshelves around our house. We thought a lot about *Star Wars*-inspired recipes until we landed on this fun assortment of drinks where the sparkling water represents the stars in the *Star Wars* galaxy and each of the additions creates a little nod to our favorite *Star Wars* characters. The fruits, vegetables, and herbs infuse into the water, making your daily water intake a creative and imaginative endeavor.

Ingredients

Sparkling water

½ medium cucumber, thinly sliced

4–5 mint leaves, roughly chopped

5–10 blueberries, sliced in half

5–10 blackberries, sliced in half

½ lemon, cut into thick slices

½ orange, cut into thick slices

Directions

1. Pour the sparkling water into five small pitchers or large glasses.

   - **For Yoda water,** add cucumbers or mint (or both!).
   - **For Luke Skywalker water,** add blueberries.
   - **For Darth Vader water,** add blackberries.
   - **For C3PO water,** add lemon slices.
   - **For Ewok water,** add orange slices.

2. Let the fruits, vegetables, and herbs steep in the water for a few minutes before serving. Line up the pitchers or glasses side by side for a full *Star Wars* cast.

Flavored sparkling water inspired by *Star Wars*
by George Lucas

IDEA JUICE

Serves 2–3 | **Medium** | *Adventurous* | **AA | GF | K | V | VE**

What Do You Do With an Idea? is a book about following your dreams. It's about thinking big and seeing those big thoughts through. With a healthy green juice made of ingredients to boost your mind and body, anything you can imagine is possible.

Ingredients

1–2 kale leaves, washed and trimmed, with the rough stalks at the bottom discarded

2 C spinach leaves, washed

½ apple, peeled and cored

½ C pineapple, peeled and cut into chunks

½ cucumber, peeled and cut into chunks

2–4 T. water, as needed

Directions

1. Combine all of the ingredients in a blender. This recipe works best if you have a juicer, Vitamix, or other high-powered blender. Blend until smooth. If the ingredients are not blending easily, add water one tablespoon at a time as needed until you reach a smooth consistency.

2. Pour the juice from the blender into a pitcher through a strainer. Depending on how fibrous the vegetables are, you may have to work it through the strainer with a spatula to get a smooth, juice-like consistency. Serve immediately and feel the ideas start to flow!

A healthy and delicious green juice inspired by *What Do You Do With an Idea?* by Kobi Yamada

"WE'RE ALL MAD HERE" TEA

Serves 2–4 | Easy | AA | D (with cream) | GF | S | V | VE (without honey or cream)

Alice in Wonderland is a beloved story in our house. It was one of my favorite stories as a child, and Poppy in particular loves the story now. One of our favorite scenes from the book is the tea party at the Mad Hatter's house. It's completely silly, totally nonsensical, a little strange, and so much fun that we went ahead and made a special tea to serve at our very own tea party.

Ingredients

8 oz. water

2 T. loose chamomile leaves or
3 chamomile tea bags

1 T. fresh mint leaves or 1 herbal mint tea bag

1 t. fresh lavender

Honey (optional)

Cream (optional)

Directions

1. Boil water in a teapot. In the meantime, place the chamomile, mint, and lavender in a heat-safe teapot or pitcher.

2. When the water comes to a boil, pour the water into the pot or pitcher and let steep for 5 to 7 minutes. Using a strainer, pour into individual teacups and serve with a touch of honey and cream, if using.

Wildly mad herbal tea inspired by *Alice in Wonderland* by Lewis Carroll

GOLDEN MILK

Serves 1 | Easy | Adventurous | AA | D | GF | S | V | VE (with non-dairy milk and without honey)

In our house, we find the story of *Rumpelstiltskin* a little scary. The main character is an angry, wild little man and he can be quite aggressive, but we love the thought of the beautiful spun gold. This warm, golden, spiced milk reminds us of that (and we're okay with not reading the story all that often).

Ingredients

1 C milk

1½ t. high-quality turmeric

1 t. cinnamon

½ t. ginger powder

½ t. orange zest (you can use tangerine, mandarin, or lemon zest in place of orange depending on what you have on hand)

½ T. honey (optional)

Directions

1. Warm the milk in a saucepan on the stove over medium heat, gently stirring occasionally so that the milk does not stick to the bottom of the pan. In the meantime, combine the turmeric, cinnamon, and ginger powder in a small bowl.

2. When the milk begins to bubble lightly, add the turmeric mixture and whisk until well-incorporated. Add the zest and honey, if using, and whisk again until well incorporated. Turn off the heat. Pour into your favorite mug and serve.

When zesting any citrus, zest the skin only, not the white pith, which is bitter. The best tool to use for this is a Microplane grater, but a small, fine grater will work too.

A sweet and spice-filled golden milk inspired by *Rumpelstiltskin* by Brothers Grimm

BON
APPÉTIT &
THE END!

ACKNOWLEDGMENTS

First and foremost, this book would never have happened but for my children, Johnny, Poppy, and Jude. Without you, I would not have had occasion to read (or re-read) all of these fantastic stories and create the recipes in this book. It is the greatest joy of my life to cook for you and care for you and be your mother, and I thank God every day for you.

Thanks also to Abe, my love, whose knife and other key skills in the kitchen have far surpassed mine (while I pretend not to notice and call out orders anyway).

Thanks to my mom and nonna for cooking through my childhood in such a way that it's just a thing in my bones. To my mom and dad for coming home from date nights at The Rex and Marius and other "it" restaurants all around Southern California in the '80s and '90s and re-counting bedside, course by course, the fabulous things you ate. I stayed up just to hear you describe your meals and I still remember some of them to this day.

Thanks to my dear friend Kate Conway and my sister Fabianne Furman for acting as first-round editors and sounding boards on this project. Fabi—you went above and beyond again and again and I can't thank you enough! A huge thanks to Alexis Douglas for support from day one. Thanks to my sister Arianne Furman for reading the *other book* (just in case it's never published and I don't get a chance to thank you publicly).

Thanks to all of my recipe testers, to Emily Temple for supporting the project, to my amazing editor Nina Spahn, and to Mascot Books for the platform and for being a really good alternative.

Thanks also from the bottom of my heart to my sisters Hannah Philpot and Briana Borten for literally bringing this book to life, and lifting me up during what should have been an impossible 24 hours that we managed to get through somehow, together. Thanks to Tara and Elisa for loyalty and sisterhood. Ali, too, since 1996. Thank you to Eden Mamushet Wordofa for caring for the kids so lovingly and cooking so many of these recipes tirelessly alongside me. A big thanks to Donna Albertson for swooping in at the last minute with a superhero cape and some fairy wings, both.

To my fabulous illustrator, Sara Brenton, who made the fairytale aspect of the recipes come to life: you are supremely talented, a hard and reliable worker, and a digital friend I am truly grateful for having met.

Finally, the kids and I would like to thank the authors of the beautiful books referenced here, who gave us inspiration for each of the recipes and the idea to put this cookbook together. The kids also want to thank "mama and papa because we love them." Johnny would like to thank Jude because "Jude made the pictures better when he was in them." Poppy would like to thank "Aunt Hannah because she made the whole cookbook because she took the pictures." Jude would like to thank "Captain Underpants tra la la!"

ABOUT THE AUTHOR

Desirée Moore is obsessed with avocados and is convinced there is a worldwide mayonnaise conspiracy that is out to get her. Her love of cooking started in childhood, where she cooked in an open kitchen filled with California sunshine alongside her Italian mother and grandmother. That love of cooking continues to this day. When she isn't whipping up a quick pasta dinner for her family or baking with her children on the weekends (*The Great British Bake Off*-style), she is a practicing lawyer in Chicago, Illinois.